Improving Practice in Continuing Education

Modern Approaches for Understanding the Field and Determining Priorities

————————————————

Jerold W. Apps

Improving Practice in Continuing Education

Jossey-Bass Publishers

San Francisco • London • 1985

IMPROVING PRACTICE IN CONTINUING EDUCATION
*Modern Approaches for Understanding the Field
and Determining Priorities*
by Jerold W. Apps

Copyright © 1985 by: Jossey-Bass Inc., Publishers
433 California Street
San Francisco, California 94104
&
Jossey-Bass Limited
28 Banner Street
London EC1Y 8QE

Library of Congress Cataloging in Publication Data

Apps, Jerold W. (date)
Improving practice in continuing education.

(The Jossey-Bass higher education series)
Bibliography: p. 209
Includes index.
1. Continuing education—United States—Case
studies. I. Title. II. Series.
LC5251.A869   1985   374'.973   85-9871
ISBN 0-87589-654-5 (alk. paper)

Manufactured in the United States of America

The paper in this book meets the guidelines for
permanence and durability of the Committee on
Production Guidelines for Book Longevity of the
Council on Library Resources.

JACKET DESIGN BY WILLI BAUM

FIRST EDITION

Code 8527

The Jossey-Bass
Higher Education Series

Consulting Editor
Adult and Continuing Education
Alan B. Knox
University of Wisconsin at Madison

Preface

Continuing education practitioners face difficult times. Administrators are increasingly concerned about budgets, income levels, number of participants, rapid turnover of teaching staffs, and competition from other continuing education providers, real or perceived. All continuing education practitioners know they must plan for the future, but they are so pressed by day-to-day concerns that they have little time for planning. Even when time is available, they often wonder how to approach such fundamental questions as: What are we really doing—as teachers of adults, as administrators, as continuing education policymakers? What do we believe we should be doing? What assumptions underlie our answers to these questions?

This book provides a systematic approach to finding answers to these and related questions. The core of the approach is a carefully developed analytic method for examining five aspects of continuing education practice: adults as learners, aims for continuing education programs, teaching and learning, content and program development, and continuing education policy decisions.

Until now, no book in continuing education has provided a comprehensive yet detailed approach for critically examining the field. Many books have been written about how to administer, plan, teach, evaluate, and promote continuing education activity. But none has focused on a critical examination of current practice as a foundation for improving future planning. A guide for systematically analyzing continuing education practice has long been needed—and this book seeks to meet that need.

This book is written for continuing education practitioners: Administrators in a variety of continuing education agencies and institutions, college and university continuing education programmers, community college instructors, vocational-technical teachers, trainers in business and industry, librarians, community development specialists, religious education directors, and consultants are examples. Policymakers in continuing education who may serve on advisory boards and who make decisions about finances, goals, and guidelines for programs should also find this book useful. The book should also appeal to graduate students seeking degrees in continuing education studies, as well as to other students in education searching for a systematic approach to analyzing education programs.

Overview of the Contents

Improving Practice in Continuing Education combines an analytic approach with case studies and other examples of application. Material for the book comes from a wide spectrum of disciplines, bringing together ideas seldom seen in continuing education books. Many readers will find the extensive bibliography useful for developing ideas further.

Chapter One describes the need for analyzing continuing education practice. It also discusses the benefits that accrue from analysis, such as helping practitioners become aware of the reasons for doing what they do and freeing them from depending on someone else's ideas. Chapter Two introduces a process for conducting a critical analysis of one's practice and presents the analytic framework that is used through the rest of the book. Chapter Three deals with identifying and analyzing assumptions, definitions, metaphors, and slogans. For instance, educators of adults often refer to the "growth" metaphor ("We look for growth in our learners"). Is this always an appropriate metaphor? Does it create images that are inaccurate or inappropriate? This chapter also explains how to ask fundamental questions and examine the arguments presented in continuing education reports and other writings.

Chapter Four looks at continuing education broadly, drawing on information from a wide array of disciplines such as psychology, sociology, anthropology, history, phenomenology, philosophy, and physics. This broad approach allows one to evaluate continuing education practice from a variety of perspectives. Chapter Four also introduces "What should be?" questions for continuing education: What should be its aims? What should be the programming approaches followed? What should be one's view of the adult as learner?

Chapter Five presents various perspectives on the adult as learner and encourages practitioners to analyze their own views on this topic. Believing that adult learners are proactive rather than passive motivates the educator to develop self-directed learning materials, to provide for discussion and other interactive learning, and to place considerable responsibility on the learner rather than on the educator.

Chapter Six illustrates how the aims and goals of continuing education can be examined. Following the examples in this chapter, practitioners will be able to analyze the aims of their organization or agency, indeed the aims of the field. Practitioners are then challenged to reconsider which aims are worth pursuing: To what extent should continuing education be involved in social action programming, in programming to meet individual needs, and in meeting the needs of a community? To what extent should continuing education provide broad liberal arts programming and make available remedial programs such as literacy training and effective writing? Several aims are often present within a single agency or institution. Examining aims and their relationships to each other can be useful in making decisions about budgets, staffing, programming, and orientation.

Chapter Seven includes examples of how teaching approaches, including the use of computers and other educational technology, can be evaluated and understood in continuing education. Such analysis can assist practitioners in making informed choices about which approaches they should use and in understanding the implications of their choices. For instance, an analysis of computer-assisted instruction reveals that some programs are highly directive, with learners given preselected choices for responding to questions. In other programs, learners are offered simulations of real situations and much greater opportunity for a creative response. Relating an understanding of adults as learners to these situations helps practitioners see which choice is more apt to result in in-depth learning and satisfied learners.

Chapter Eight explores the age-old questions, "What should be taught, who decides, and how is it decided?" By following the procedures introduced in this chapter, practitioners will be able to examine program development strategies in a new light and to broaden the programming approaches they use.

Chapter Nine focuses on policy statements in continuing education. This chapter also includes several challenges for practitioners and policymakers in continuing education: developing a vision and a sense of the future; more clearly defining the purposes of continuing education programming; relating continuing education to elementary, secondary, and postsecondary education; and seeing the value of the many settings and approaches to continuing education, including the importance of self-directed learning.

The book is designed as a practical guide, focusing on the problems and concerns that practitioners face in their day-to-day responsibilities. But rather than offering a single simplistic answer, this book presents approaches to analyzing questions and problems, with suggested alternatives and options.

Acknowledgments

Several people helped me with this book. I particularly want to thank Timothy Turner, research assistant, for the many hours he spent locating references and providing editorial criticism at every stage of the project. Alan B. Knox, professor of continuing education at the University of Wisconsin at Madison; M. Donald Campbell, director, Office of Extended Education,

University of Wisconsin at LaCrosse; Ronald Podeschi, associate professor, cultural foundations of education, University of Wisconsin at Milwaukee; and Dušan Savićević, professor of andragogy, University of Belgrade, Yugoslavia, read the entire manuscript and offered many suggestions for improvement. Quentin H. Gessner, dean, continuing studies, University of Nebraska, and Philip Nowlen, executive director, continuing education programs, the University of Chicago, read one of the case studies and suggested important changes. Several colleagues in my department, Sara Steele, Boyd Rossing, and Laverne Forest, critiqued sections of the manuscript and made valuable comments. And, lastly, I want especially to thank Frances Pauley who guided the many drafts of this manuscript through the word processor.

Madison, Wisconsin   Jerold W. Apps
May 1985

Contents

The Author

Jerold W. Apps is professor of continuing education and chairperson of the Department of Continuing and Vocational Education at the University of Wisconsin at Madison. He received his B.S. degree (1955), his M.S. degree (1957), and his Ph.D. (1967) all from the University of Wisconsin. His doctorate is in adult education.

Apps's research has focused on obstacles to learning faced by adults returning to the college classroom and on the application of philosophy to continuing education. In 1982 he won the Research to Practice Award presented by the Adult Education Association of the United States for his research on applying philosophy to continuing education practice. Apps's books include *Toward a Working Philosophy of Adult Education* (1973), *How to Improve Adult Education in Your Church* (1972), *Problems in Continuing Education* (1979), *Study Skills for Adults Returning to School* (1978, 1982), *Redefining the Discipline of Adult Education* (1980, with Robert D. Boyd), *The Adult Learner on Campus* (1981), and *Improving Your Writing Skills* (1982).

xvii

Other universities where Apps has taught credit classes and led workshops on applying philosophy to continuing education include the University of Alberta, Edmonton; University of Quelph, Ontario; North Carolina State University; the University of Georgia; the University of Minnesota; and the University of Illinois.

Improving Practice in Continuing Education

Modern Approaches for Understanding the Field and Determining Priorities

1

Benefits of Analyzing
Priorities and Practices

~~~~~~

As I travel around the country trying to listen carefully to what continuing education practitioners are saying, I hear a variety of messages. Continuing education administrators are concerned about budgets and keeping them balanced. They are concerned about the rapid turnover of their staffs and the constant need to orient new staff members to approaches for teaching adults. "How can I improve marketing strategies for my program offerings?" is a question asked by many administrators. This question, of course, concerns how to keep enrollment numbers up. A related question, which is sometimes not spoken aloud, is "How can I compete with the array of other continuing education providers operating in my area?"

Many continuing education administrators are concerned about future directions for the field, but they are frustrated with the many day-to-day pressures that prevent them from considering more long-range questions. A director of a continuing education program at a small private college said, "I am so busy keeping everything going, promoting my programs, balancing my budget, trying to convince the college's vice-president that I need more help that there is no time for long-range plan-

1

ning. No time at all. I worry about today, there's no time to even think about tomorrow. All I can hope for is to survive. And I should do long-range planning? When?"

"I'm becoming increasingly more cynical," another practitioner said to me at a national continuing education conference. "Knowledge has become something that is bought and sold like hamburger. I feel like a meat cutter. I take a hunk of knowledge, cut it up and wrap it in a nice package, and run an ad that says, 'Buy my knowledge,' and I hope to make a little profit on the transaction so I can keep the meat market open. Have we moved too far in making knowledge a commodity to be bought and sold? What about the thousands of people who can't afford our knowledge? Do we have any obligation to them?"

Sitting in on a group discussing the future direction for college and university continuing education, I heard a series of comments. A political scientist offered, "Society is changing so fast these days that I'm afraid our continuing education programs are hopelessly out of date. We are programming as if it were yesterday, not tomorrow."

A former general extension dean added, "When we think broadly, when we think about the world—and we must begin doing that—we see problems of world hunger, of economic disparity, of a threat of nuclear war. Where do our continuing education programs fit? Do they have anything to contribute to solving these global problems?"

A German professor broke into the conversation: "I see a need for our college and university continuing education programs to spend more time focusing on problems—but taking a broader approach than we have in the past. It seems to me we must combine technological solutions to problems with humanistic perspectives. I'm afraid we are serving up technological answers—computers, high technology, for example—without examining the humanistic side. In fact, I'd like to ask a fundamental question: Do programs in the arts and humanities have any future in a society that appears driven by economic and materialistic concerns?"

"I'm concerned about the way we finance continuing

education," a university administrator commented. "With our present system, the consumer pays the total cost or near total cost through fees. Thus we must provide programs that 'sell.' Where is there room for innovation, for experimentation? How do we test new ideas? Where do we get the money?"

At a state meeting of continuing education practitioners representing a broad range of providers, I heard: "I'm convinced that quality must come before quantity, but I'm forced to keep increasing enrollments and keep my income level high. I'm wondering whether quality doesn't end up in second place with these pressures."

A young woman stood up in the back of the room and said, "We are talking about lifelong learning today—that's what we say we are talking about. But aren't we really talking about lifelong attending? Just listen to us, to the words we use: 'reaching the hard to reach,' 'increasing participation through improved marketing'—these are words that assume participation. Does somebody have to attend something to learn something?"

Another hand shot up, and this question was posed: "As we change from a postindustrial to an information society (à la Naisbitt's *Megatrends*), what do we do differently with our continuing education programs?"

In the lobby, around the coffee pot, the questions and comments after the formal presentation filled the air. A longtime practitioner mused, "How much of our programming should be that which no participant or potential participant has ever mentioned, ever asked about? Do we have a responsibility for stretching minds, for offering programs that will get people to think about things they have never thought about before, programs that will challenge their values and the values of society? Can we risk this kind of programming? Can we afford not to risk it?"

The continuing education practitioner can be compared to a canoeist paddling in a river. At times the river is flat and smooth and we paddle with little effort. At other times the stream rushes through steep-sided gorges, hurtles around hairpin turns, and slams over rocky rapids. At these moments we paddle furiously, trying to keep the canoe afloat and headed in the same direction as the cascading water. We devote our entire attention to the immediate situation, for one tiny error and the canoe would be swamped and we and the other occupants would be tossed into the swirling water. Once through the rapids, the river becomes smooth and tranquil. We relax and enjoy the scenery, we appreciate the shade of the great trees that line the river's edge, we observe the beaver, otter, deer, and other wildlife often found near running water.

In some sections of the river, we come onto so many other canoes there is scarcely room to thrust a paddle into the water. Occasionally one canoe will bump into another, and angry words are spoken about finding another river or at least learning to paddle a truer course.

Sometimes we tire of paddling in the fast-moving water and stop, allowing the current to move the canoe as it will, this way and that, bouncing off this bank and then the other. But the river is unrelenting; the unguided canoe becomes beached on a pebble-strewn shore or caught on a rock in midstream, the rushing water moving around and past, leaving the canoe and its occupants behind.

We may decide that we cannot face the river anymore and put in on shore, tie the canoe to a tree, and watch the river and the other canoes float by. Perhaps later we decide to push off once more but discover the river has changed: Although it appears the same from a distance, it is not; the currents shift, the sandbars move, and the channel is constantly adjusting.

Paddling along, we often face a fork in the river, where the main channel appears to split and go in two directions. Usually there is little evidence to suggest which branch is the actual channel and which one will lead into the mudflats and marshes where there is eventually too little water to keep the canoe afloat. If we choose the wrong channel from time to time, and we all do, the tendency is to work frantically to turn the canoe around, return to the main channel, and resume paddling. But sometimes we are stuck so badly that we cannot easily turn around, and in our quandary we begin thinking, asking ourselves questions. At first the questions apply to the immediate situation: How did I get into this mess? Who or what can help me out of it? Later I may ask: Should I buy a different canoe, one that floats more easily in shallow water? Should I look for some new maps that more accurately tell me which fork of the river is the true channel? Should I learn how to better read the river so I do not end up in a predicament like this again? The questions often give way to broader ones. Am I paddling in the right river? Do I have the most up-to-date paddles? Should I consider buying a motor for my canoe? Are there new approaches to paddling that I should learn, new techniques for turning, for shooting rapids? Is there a way of packing my canoe more efficiently so it will move quickly and quietly but carry more cargo with the same or less effort? Sometimes we ask even broader questions: Should I sell my canoe and purchase a rowboat, or a kayak, or maybe a rubber life raft? Or should I leave the river business entirely and become a diesel truck driver?

It is not difficult to equate a continuing education program with a canoe and the practitioner with the canoeist. The practitioner and the canoeist face similar challenges. There is another similarity as well. Unfortunately, like the canoeist, we practitioners in continuing education often do not ask the more penetrating questions about our practice until we face some type of difficulty or a near-crisis situation. We paddle along from day to day, accepting our work with its challenges and not taking time to examine or question what we do and what are the outcomes of our efforts. But many practitioners are facing difficult times, and they are asking questions and expressing concern.

I plan to discuss these questions and many more like them in this book. My approach does not emphasize an immediate search for answers. Indeed, in many instances my emphasis is on asking new and different questions and then exploring alternative answers.

I believe that all of us who are practitioners in continuing education must, from time to time, reflect on our practice and ask penetrating questions. We must, I believe, learn how to systematically analyze what we do and how and why we do it and to reflect on the outcomes of our efforts. To go back to the story about the stream, we must, from time to time, pull the canoe up on shore and reflect on where we are, where we have been, and where we want to go. Oftentimes, you may argue, that is impossible to do. The canoe must continue downstream. If that is the case, then let someone else paddle for a while so you have time to reflect and question.

Contributions of Analysis to the Practitioner

Analysis helps us, first, to become aware of what we do as practitioners, including being able to see our experience in a fresh way. When we analyze our practice, we step back from it and gain a new perspective. Second, analysis shows us alternative approaches for planning programs, organizing workshops, teaching classes, promoting, budgeting, and the host of other functions that are a part of what we do. Third, analysis helps us become aware of values, ethics, and esthetics as applied to continuing education. We must always ask: Is this approach ethical? Is this procedure morally sound? Have I considered the esthetics of this situation? Again, these matters will be explored in greater depth later in the book. But for now, it is important to realize that these questions are often not raised.

I recall a few years ago when I was working with another person on a planned book about ethics and the education of adults. My partner received a small grant from our publisher to visit several continuing education institutions and agencies to discuss with educators there how they made ethical decisions in their day-to-day work. He asked these practitioners how important they felt ethics were for their operations. And finally, he asked them whether they felt a book about ethics, with some guidelines about ethical decision making, might be of value.

We were surprised and somewhat appalled by the responses he collected. All agreed that ethics were relevant in their operations, but meeting their budget was more important. They conceded that although they believed ethics were relevant, they gave little thought to them. They also said they believed that there were few if any problems concerning ethics in the field of continuing education and that a book was not necessary. We did not write the book. But I have since given considerable thought to the responses we received from respected educators of adults. I am not suggesting that the general practice of educating adults is unethical. But to believe that there are no problems with ethics is irresponsible.

What has esthetics to do with the education of adults, particularly if we are talking about programs and activities outside the arts? Does not esthetics belong to the arts? Certainly it does, but not exclusively. Designing educational programs for adults that have inherent beauty to them by virtue of the way they are organized is one way we can apply esthetics. Giving attention to the amenities that go along with educational programs, properly spaced breaks, pleasant surroundings (this does not mean a plush conference center—a tent pitched by a rushing stream is a pleasant surrounding), and variety of activities is another way we can apply esthetics. Of course, we may also offer courses in the arts that have esthetics as content.

Fourth, following analytic approaches, we can become aware of our own personal histories and their influence on our role as educators of adults. It is easy to become caught up with the pressures of the present, so that we reflect little on the future and reflect seldom, if at all, on the past. Yet, much of what we are as human beings is a product of our histories, where we were born, where we grew up, where we went to school, who our friends were, who was our first lover. Who we are today is a subtle mixture of all these forces, and they influence how we think and what we do as educators of adults. An analysis helps us become aware of our past in a way that goes beyond nostalgia.

And finally, analysis can free us from depending on someone else's doctrine. It can empower us to make critical choices, to choose the direction in which we wish to go as educators of adults. By using analytic tools, we, as continuing education practitioners, can become autonomous individuals with the confidence to challenge and question the existing doctrines of the field and of our agencies and institutions. This is not to say that we will reject all the existing doctrines, although some we will likely reject. But when we subscribe to a doctrine that we have examined, we are subscribing to it thoughtfully, out of the knowledge that we understand it and can accept it.

For the individual educator of adults and for administrators and policy makers, this contribution of analysis is extremely powerful and fundamental. It raises the basic question of the role of practitioners and their right to think and challenge, rather than a subservient role of always following someone else's direction. If this idea seems remote, reflect on how educators of adults have quickly accepted, often without questioning, approaches to program development, applications of technology in teaching, and approaches to evaluation and accountability. In succeeding chapters we will examine "doctrine" about adults as learners, about teaching and learning, about aims of continuing education, about program development, and about policy direction.

Contributions of Analysis to the Field

By following analytic approaches, we can serve the entire field of continuing education. Analysis takes the field of continuing education and examines, probes, and helps to clarify. The analytic attitude is one of encouraging comprehensive approaches to posing and examining questions. The analytic attitude encourages a search for consistency but at the same time allows for and accepts ambiguity.

Careful analysis serves as continuing education's conscience, raising questions of an ethical and moral nature about various practices and procedures. From a comprehensive perspective, analysis helps us understand the various aspects of the field, particularly the presuppositions that guide it. An analysis helps us see the relationship of the various segments of the field to the totality of the field. By analyzing, we can begin to see in overview the relationship of the aims of the field to the practices and procedures that are followed. We can see the relationship of the various views the field holds about the nature of knowledge and how it is acquired to such applied questions as the use of technology.

Analysis provides an attitude and a framework for criticizing the field. Here I am using *criticize* in the most positive sense. For any field of endeavor to maintain a sense of relevance and worthwhileness, it must constantly seek ways of criticizing itself. An analysis, by the nature of the questions asked and the procedures followed in seeking answers, can provide a framework for criticism. For instance, "What should be the aims of continuing education?" is a question that often leads to a further examination of practice.

Careful analysis assists the field by providing a means for examining the relationship of continuing education to the rest of society. Too often, it seems, the field is inclined to go its own way, to feed on its own interests, without a concern for a relationship to the rest of society. Such questions as the following are important: Which problems and concerns in society have educational dimensions and thus should be addressed by continuing education? What role should continuing education play in the prevention of problems, such as in the wellness movement that has come into prominence in recent years? What role should continuing education play in social change, perhaps working in concert with various citizen groups in communities?

Obstacles to Analysis

If we can see no reason for analyzing our practice, can see no value from the effort, then we obviously will not become involved. Most of us, as we do our work from day to day, become comfortable. Our experience helps us to do what we do in a near-routine fashion. This is important, for few of us have the physical and emotional energy to face each day with everything new and filled with surprises.

But there are dangers that accompany comfort. Comfortableness leads to complacency, and complacency puts blinders on our peripheral vision. That sharp edge we had when we first came to our job becomes dulled, and we are less open to the various changes that are going on around us. We may not even notice the changes because of our mind set. The first thing in analyzing is to realize that we are wearing blinders, that we must begin to look at what we do in new and fresh ways.

We are often motivated to analyze our practice because we are uncomfortable in our work; something is wrong, we do not feel right about what we are doing, but we cannot put our finger on what it is exactly. Or we may be receiving more criticism than we ordinarily do, with suggestions that changes may be necessary, but we do not know what the changes should be.

We may feel just the opposite about our work. There are no problems, everything is going well. We are feeling secure. Often these "good times" can pose the greatest problems for us, because our good feelings may be hiding problems that we are not able to see. We must learn how to change the usual to the unusual so we can see what we are doing in a new light. We must force ourselves to examine, to question, to probe, to make what is comfortable uncomfortable.

For some practitioners, particularly those who are administrators, day-to-day tasks have kept them so busy they believe they do not have time to consider something that appears one step (or several steps) removed from the pressures they feel every day. Broudy (1955) wrote, "To some educational administrators education has become equivalent to budgets, . . . board meetings, building programs, and the hiring and firing of faculty. The 'big time' educators in our time are more likely to resemble a 'big time' manager or promoter than an intellectual of any stripe. Such [administrators] hold theory of any kind suspect unless it leads to immediate results in terms of budget, enrollments, salaries, and similar marks of institutional prosperity" (p. 620).

Many practitioners believe that science will provide the answers to their questions and that carefully designed research projects, following sound scientific methods, will eventually solve their problems. Because money and time for research are lacking, many of the problems that educators face today have not been solved. But when resources become available, these educators believe, their problems will be solved. These same educators, who have this strong faith in the values of science, fail to credit the approach to analysis presented here (with roots in philosophy) as relevant to solving problems. If a problem cannot be solved scientifically, it probably cannot be solved, they believe.

Some problems faced by educators could be solved if more money were available for research and more researchers could be turned loose on these problems. But even with adequate resources, science, by virtue of the kinds of questions it asks and the kinds of procedures it follows, cannot solve all the problems that continuing education faces. Science cannot address problems that involve value judgments such as the ethics and morality of educational behavior. Although science often addresses the question of prediction, it cannot and does not address the normative question of "what should be."

When analyzing practice following procedures in this book, one will often encounter a variety of responses. For those seeking single answers, multiple, sometimes contradictory responses can be disconcerting. One of the strengths of analyzing practice in this way is that it opens doors to alternative ways of viewing situations. Rather than seeking a single answer, such an analysis probes a situation and often comes up with a variety of responses, depending on the person examining the question.

Lastly, some continuing education practitioners firmly subscribe to specialization and believe that specialists in analysis such as educational philosophers should analyze educational problems. This is not my position. I believe everyone can do analysis of continuing education, particularly continuing education practitioners. That is not to negate the role of professional educational philosophers. They most certainly have a role, but not an exclusive one.

Empowering the Continuing Education Practitioner

Many years ago, as scholars and researchers began to define what we today call the disciplines—physics, mathematics, history, sociology, biology, philosophy, and so on—the era of specialization began. With specialization came an attitude that one must stay within one's discipline if serious inquiry and study were to be attempted.

We all know that the majority of the people in the world, though aware of the disciplines and the specialists who work within them, are not concerned with the tightly defined areas of specialization. If one's task required mathematics, one used it;

if historical information seemed appropriate, whether for a pragmatic use or simply for pleasure, one obtained it. If some principles from the study of plants and animals were appropriate to something being done, one consulted that discipline.

The specialists who saw themselves as responsible for the new knowledge in the disciplines and for the dissemination of that knowledge believed they were making major contributions to society by giving to "ordinary folks" the information that they wanted. As the years passed, many of the "ordinary folks" often became dissatisfied with the information they received from these discipline specialists. Either it was "packaged" in a way they could not understand—incomprehensible writing, excessive jargon—or the information did not fit the situation at hand. Sometimes other reasons for rejection were offered as well. Some people simply did not believe the information they were receiving. Sometimes there was concern that the information lacked a moral quality—a person received a recommendation to use a particular chemical on a plant pest, for example, but little or no advice was available about side effects. Too often so much information was provided that the person simply could not decide what was important and what was not.

Increasingly, "ordinary folks," people like you and me, began to do their own science and their own history. In a way this was a return to a time that existed before the era of disciplines and narrow specializations when people inquired into many areas to find information.

All this is not to discount specialists and disciplines. Indeed not. But because we have people who can tell us about the sociology of continuing education, about the psychology of adult learning, and about philosophical positions in the field, we should not—must not—become dependent on them for our information. We must do some of our own sociology, some of our own psychology, some of our own historical investigation, and some of our own philosophy.

Our task is to blend our own information, that which we have gathered from our own investigations, with that we have obtained from the specialists. We are thus in control and are less dependent on specialists.

Each of us is able to do an analysis of his or her practice with a philosophical perspective. Granted, there are various levels. The scholar in philosophy who has spent a lifetime in the field works at it differently than a continuing education practitioner interested in making sense out of some aspect of what he or she does. That does not make what the specialist in philosophy does better than what you or I might do. It just makes it different.

In one sense we cannot avoid doing analysis. We do it every day of our lives. When we wonder about who we are, about what we are accomplishing, about our goals and dreams, we are doing an analysis. When we think about the effects of our teaching, about how we are or are not influencing people, about what right we have to try to change someone else, we are doing analysis. We are doing analysis when we confront ourselves with what we believe about life, about work, about play, about relationships. We are doing analysis when we examine what is significant, what is ethical, what is valuable, and what is beautiful. Analyzing is a part of living. My premise here is that although we are doing it, we can do it better, in more depth, in a broader way.

Analysis and Philosophy

As I mentioned earlier, the approach to analysis that I am offering has its roots in philosophy. Dictionary definitions of *analysis* usually refer to examining the relationship of the parts of something to one another. Analysis, as I use the term, goes much further. My use of the term *analysis* draws on that segment of philosophy most often called "philosophical inquiry" or "philosophizing." Some readers may wish to substitute *philosophical inquiry* or *philosophizing* for *analysis* and *analyzing*, the terms I will use most often in this book.

In what ways does analysis, as I am using the term, relate to philosophical inquiry? Let us examine what several writers have said about philosophy.

Langer (1956) writes, "Philosophy is the establishment of coherent meanings in the whole domain of thought" (p. 139).

Smith (1978) emphasizes philosophy's interest in such basic issues as existence, the nature of human nature, differences between appearances and reality, standards of good and evil, the nature of truth, beauty, and justice. He points out philosophy's interest in raising questions, the meaning of key terms, identifying basic principles and assumptions, conceptual relationships, methods of reasoning, and standards of evaluation (pp. 1-6).

Lyons (1982) suggests, "Philosophy . . . is not neutrally descriptive of the universe and its moving parts. It does not set out merely to describe the items in the universe and how they interact according to causal law. Philosophy sets out deliberately to question the very methods of finding out about the nature of the universe and, which is more worrying to the doctrinal doorkeepers, to question not merely the methods and claimed results of the social planner and political programmer [and all other aspects of continuing education as well], but the purpose and worth of the plans and programmes themselves" (pp. 228-229).

Barnett (1981) says, "Philosophy challenges us to evaluate the competence of our own reasoning" (p. 8). He goes on to suggest that the first question raised by the philosopher is "Do you know what you are doing in using a personal standard of competence to decide what deserves your attention and what you may safely ignore?" (p. 9). "What the philosopher proposes is that we inquire into the limits of our understanding and conscious agency and seek to discover what we have been committing ourselves to, what we have been believing and doing which extends beyond those limits" (p. 12).

Reid (1972) suggests, "Philosophy includes digging up and criticizing one's assumptions, one's experiences and one's judgments in all the main fields of human enterprise. . . . All this involves an examination of ideas and of the language (and languages) in which they are expressed, scrutinizing for ambiguity, exploring meanings" (p. 23).

Harris (1960) emphasizes the importance of raising questions. Examples of questions are: What is education? What is knowledge? What knowledge is of most worth? How is human nature to be conceived? What should be the educational program? And by what criteria are educational judgments made?

And finally, "Philosophy may be regarded as a way of approaching (or looking at or taking a stance with respect to) the knowledge gained by the natural and human sciences, the awarenesses made possible by the arts, and the personal insights into existence each human being accumulates as he lives. Philosophy is a way of framing distinctive sorts of questions having to do with what is presupposed, perceived, intuited, believed, and known. It is a way of contemplating, examining, or thinking about what is taken to be significant, valuable, beautiful, worthy of commitment. It is a way of becoming self-aware, of constituting meanings in one's life-world. Critical thinking is demanded, as are deliberate attempts to make things clear" (Greene, 1973, p. 7).

Throughout this book analysis includes the functions of philosophy as described above. It also includes a sense of wonder, an attitude of concern, and a quest for understanding. When we ask "Why?" and "What should be?," we are asking analytic questions. When we search for assumptions undergirding our teaching practice, when we seek careful definitions, try to understand metaphors and slogans, or examine the logic of an argument, when we question, challenge, probe, and seek understanding, we are doing analysis. Analysis is taking apart and putting together—examining a position statement from several perspectives, dissecting the statement into its component parts, then reassembling the statement into something that says more than the pieces alone can provide.

Analysis can be broad and abstract or narrow and specific. It can examine a question such as: What is the purpose of continuing education? It can also examine the meaning of the word *need.*

Analysis includes history and future. It can include science and art. It can be pursued by specially trained professional philosophers, but concerned educators of adults, with little or no training in philosophy, can also do analysis.

Summary

Busy practitioners in continuing education often do not take the time to step back and examine where they have been, where they are, and where they wish to go. Yet, such a systematic analysis can often improve practice and make the practitioner's job more enjoyable.

Analysis can assist continuing education practitioners in several ways. It can help us become critically aware of what we do as practitioners; show us alternative approaches to program planning, teaching, budgeting, and so on; help us become aware of how values, ethics, and esthetics can be applied to continuing education practice; illustrate to us the importance of our personal histories and how they influence what we do as educators; and free us from dependence on someone else's doctrine.

A systematic analysis of continuing education practice can also serve the field by insisting that the field's premises are sound; by serving as a conscience for the field by raising ethical and moral questions; by assisting in understanding the field from several perspectives, including seeing the relationship of continuing education to other fields and to society in general; and by providing an attitude and framework for criticizing the field.

Unfortunately, a systematic analysis of practice often does not occur, because practitioners do not see the value of such activity, because they are comfortable in what they are doing, because day-to-day tasks consume so much time that there is none left for analysis, because they believe that scientific research will solve their problems, or because they believe systematic analysis of practice is the responsibility of a specialist.

Analysis, as used in this book, has its roots in philosophy. The term *philosophy* is often used to describe established practice, as in "The philosophy of this organization is . . ." A different dimension of philosophy serves as the basis for analysis, that of philosophical inquiry. Philosophical inquiry is concerned with going to the heart of matters, looking for basic assumptions, principles, conceptual relationships, methods of reasoning, and standards of evaluation. Once these perspectives are identified, philosophical inquiry includes a systematic examination and careful criticism of them. Philosophical inquiry also includes raising questions such as: What is the purpose of continuing education? Whom should continuing education serve, and what information is of most worth? The process of analyzing continuing education practice discussed in this book draws on the foregoing approaches to philosophical inquiry.

It is the premise of this book that every continuing education practitioner has the responsibility for analyzing his or her practice and, with some assistance, is capable of doing so.

2

Developing a Systematic
Approach to Analysis

~~~~~~

What activities can we as continuing education practitioners pursue that will assist us in analyzing our practice?

Activities

Reading. Obvious as this suggestion sounds, most of us are so busy that we read little beyond the requirements of our work. (Often the reading requirement of our jobs is so heavy we have little time or energy for additional reading.) But to begin seeing what we do in a different light, reading is a necessity. What to read? The popular nonfiction material of the day is one suggestion—what is the public reading, what is influencing public opinion? Most of us are doing this type of reading now, to a greater or lesser extent. Another suggestion is the popular fiction of the day, the novels that appear on the best-seller lists and those that do not. Often popular fiction describes better the conditions of the present time than does nonfiction, for it explores people's feelings and passions, it develops in some depth an understanding of the current state of the human condition.

Participating in the Arts. Reading poetry and fiction is one way to participate in the arts. But attending musical events, viewing quality films, visiting art galleries, and going to the theater, though often viewed as entertainment, can help one broaden perspective. The arts can help us confront ourselves with ourselves. We, of course, do this when we analyze our practice. When we examine a question such as "What is the nature of the adult as learner?," we of necessity are asking that question of ourselves. Even if we try to be "objective" in our search for an answer, we are still influenced in one way or another by what we think of ourselves as learners.

The arts are concerned with the human condition, with the emotions of living, with joy and sorrow, with love and hate, with beauty and squalor. To do a comprehensive analysis, we must ultimately consider the entirety of human existence. The arts can help us do that.

Thinking. Reflecting on what we read, what we experience, what we do in our roles as educators of adults is a key activity. When we analyze, we use at least three kinds of thinking: (1) creative thinking, which allows us to generate new ideas, consider new possibilities, invent unique combinations, speculate about new directions, (2) critical thinking, which helps us to evaluate, test, and try out the products of our creative thinking activities as well as those of others, and (3) problem solving, which assists us in working out solutions to the many problems we face in our day-to-day activities, those of a philosophical nature as well as others. John Dewey, an educational philosopher, suggested two phases in the problem-solving process (which he called reflective thinking): "(a) a state of doubt, hesitation, perplexity, mental difficulty, in which thinking originates, and (b) an act of searching, hunting, inquiring, to find material that will resolve the doubt, settle and dispose of the perplexity" (Dewey, 1933, p. 12). For Dewey, problem solving (reflective thought) "involves not simply a sequence of ideas, but a *con*-sequence—a consecutive ordering in such a way that each determines the next as its proper outcome, while each outcome in turn leans back on, or refers to, its predecessors. The successive portions of a reflective thought grow out of one another and support one another; they do not come and go in a medley" (pp. 4-5).

Creative thinking also has phases, and they overlap each other. The activities carried out within each phase are not so clearly defined as in Dewey's reflective thought. Wallas (1926, pp. 80-81) suggested the following phases for creative thinking: preparation, incubation, illumination, and verification.

During the preparation stage a person becomes immersed in the situation about which some solution or understanding is sought. One reads about the situation, reflects on the experience, or seeks out an experience—in effect, learns as much as possible about the situation. This can be a frustrating time because although much information is obtained, it often makes little sense and the pieces seldom seem to fit together. Some people have difficulty in letting the process occur; they try to make sense out of the information before the incubation period is allowed to occur. During the incubation period, the person doing creative thinking leaves the situation at hand and does something else. This allows the unconscious to work on the store of information and reflections accumulated. The illumination phase is the "aha" time, when a flash of insight pops into a person's head that reveals a solution to the problem or some new understanding. Verification is checking to see whether the solution to the problem works or whether the understanding of the situation really makes as much sense as we think.

Unfortunately, the process does not always work as suggested above. We may immerse ourselves in a situation and allow time for incubation—and no insight comes. This is the risk the creative thinker takes.

Sometimes critical thinking is confused with problem solving and even considered to be the same. But whereas problem solving is concerned with a progressive narrowing process as the solution to a problem is sought, critical thinking is an expanding, exploratory process. In fact, an outcome of critical thinking is a realization that not all problems can be solved and not all questions answered. Critical thinking is an important dimension of critical analysis (see Chapter Three).

Beyond the skills of creative, critical, and problem-solving thinking, we must become independent thinkers. We may believe we are independent thinkers, but several years on a job often deludes us into believing that we are independent thinkers when we really are not. As Krishnamurti (1953) points out, "Conventional education makes independent thinking extremely difficult. Conformity leads to mediocrity. To be different from the group . . . is not easy and is often risky as long as we worship success. The urge to be successful, which is the pursuit of reward whether in the material or in the so-called spiritual sphere, the search for inward or outward security, the desire for comfort—this whole process smothers discontent, puts an end to spontaneity, and breeds fear; and fear blocks the intelligent understanding of life" (pp. 9–10).

There are several activities we can follow that can restore our ability as independent thinkers. A simple one is to pay attention. Paying attention means to be attentive with all the senses. For example, sit under a pine tree in summer and concentrate on the sounds you hear. The wind rustling the pine needles creates a unique sound. Do the same thing while sitting under an aspen tree, and the sounds are quite different. But the key is paying attention to the sounds. Let us take the analogy a bit further: Sit under the pine tree and listen, look, be aware of your feelings, the smell in the area, perhaps even taste a pine needle. Concentrate on "paying attention" to what your senses are telling you. I have often been amazed, when I have done this, how much more I am able to "see" in a situation that on the surface appears mundane and without interest.

We can follow the same procedure with our role as continuing education practitioners. By making a special effort to pay attention, we will "see" aspects of what we do and what others do that we have not noticed before. Krishnamurti (1974) admonishes us "to learn never to accept anything which you yourself do not see clearly, never to repeat what another has said. . . . Which means you have to be extraordinarily critical" (p. 18). Once we begin to see, we often begin to question, which is the first step in analyzing.

Writing. Although writing is not a requirement for doing an analysis, putting our thoughts on paper offers several advantages. There is also a close connection between thinking and writing. Sometimes the process of writing itself helps to clarify thinking. For instance, there may be times when we really do not know what we believe about a certain situation until we start writing about it. During the writing process, ideas come into focus and we have a much clearer notion of what our thoughts are. Moreover, we have a record that we can refer to. Often ideas once clarified and not written are forgotten, never to be retrieved. It has happened to all of us.

Writing also pushes us to think more deeply, often allowing our unconscious to be called on for depths of meaning we sometimes do not even realize we had. When we begin writing our philosophical thoughts about what we do as educators of adults, we are often surprised at what results, sometimes even wondering about the source of the information. Thus thinking without writing is usually incomplete (Apps, 1982, p. 12).

A practical suggestion that many practitioners find useful, particularly those with substantial administrative responsibilities, is to keep a journal. Writing down each day insights that have occurred or describing situations that have been particularly frustrating can often help one see situations more clearly.

Discussing. The time-honored activity for gaining insights on ideas has been discussion. An idea is presented, it is challenged by another person, perhaps added to, sometimes agreed with, and occasionally dismissed. But during the process of discussing our ideas about such matters as programming in controversial areas or devising new marketing strategies or attempting to reach new audiences, we can clarify our thinking. It often takes the probing question of a friend for us to realize we had missed some important point or had not seen that our logic was faulty or that we could not defend our conclusions.

For a discussion to be fruitful, some ground rules must be followed. Too often, it seems, when we have an idea to discuss with someone, we believe our purpose is to convince that person that we are right and he or she is wrong or at least that we are more right than the other person is. So what could be a rich give-and-take degenerates into a contest to see who can win. That is not to say that a discussion should not be lively or that you should not try to make your point. But the discussion is far more valuable if its tone is to present ideas that can be challenged for the purpose of clarification, not for the purpose of proving who is right and who is wrong. It may very well be that the person with whom you are discussing believes as strongly about his or her position as you do, even though the position may be quite different from yours.

It is to your advantage if the person you are talking with happens to believe differently than you do. Recognizing an alternative to what you believe is one of the best ways to strengthen and clarify what you do believe.

Acting. Committing oneself to some sort of action as a result of doing an analysis of one's practice moves the activity away from merely an intellectual one to one that results in some sort of change in what we do. The field of continuing education is an applied field, and we are interested in improving practice. The application may be accomplished individually, it may be something that a person attempts with a small group, or it may mean becoming a part of a larger effort. But activity should result. Reflection on this activity feeds back into the other activities I have described. That is, we may think about what we have done, we may put our thoughts down on paper, or we may discuss our efforts with a friend.

To summarize, when we analyze our practice, we use skills that are common in everyday living. We read, explore our inner feelings through participating in the arts, think about what we do, how we do it, and what we believe we should be doing, we write down our thoughts, which usually helps to clarify them, we discuss what we are thinking with someone to further clarify, and we take some action based on our efforts.

Many continuing education practitioners have also found the process of analyzing personal beliefs useful in analyzing practice.

Investigating Personal Beliefs

Although some writers attempt to make analysis objective and impersonal, it is an impossible task. Analyzing continuing education is personal. How we do an analysis is wrapped up in who we are and what we believe. So one useful activity is to sort out what we believe, personally, about continuing education. Doing this puts us in a much more informed position to do further analysis of the field. My book *Toward a Working Philosophy of Adult Education* (Apps, 1973) describes in some detail a process and framework for analyzing personal beliefs. Briefly, a belief analysis process includes four phases:

1. Identifying beliefs held about continuing education—that is, beliefs about the adult learner, about the purposes for continuing education agencies and institutions, about the teaching/learning process, and about content in adult education programs. At one level it is fairly easy to list our beliefs in these various areas. But at another level it is nearly impossible, for all of us hold what are called zero-order beliefs. Zero-order beliefs are those that are so much a part of us that we do not even know we hold them. We are not aware of an alternative to such a belief. For instance, many people question the worth of anything that cannot be validated with the senses. If something cannot be seen, felt, tasted, heard, or smelled, it does not exist. Another common zero-order belief, at a more abstract level, is that all problems can be solved. What is needed, many people say, is perhaps more money, more technology, or more research, but eventually all problems can be solved. For them this is a zero-order belief.

2. Searching for contradictions among beliefs. Which beliefs do not go together, logically, even though we discover we hold them? For example, we may believe that adults learn best in programmed learning situations, yet we may also believe that adults should have freedom to learn what they wish in a way in which they want to learn. On the surface, these two beliefs appear contradictory—tightly structured learning situations versus adults' freedom to learn.

3. Discovering sources of beliefs. Two sources are most evident: experience and authority. Through our work as educators of adults, we have accumulated many beliefs about adults, adult learning, and what can be accomplished with adult education programming. Some of our beliefs result from participation in graduate courses in continuing education and in workshops

and conferences. We have also acquired beliefs from various authorities, people for whom we have worked, authors we have read, conference speakers we have heard.

For some of the beliefs we hold, we simply do not know the source. They may have come from our parents when we were children. Many of our beliefs about people in general can be traced to early childhood.

4. Making judgments about the beliefs we hold. As we identify personal beliefs and consider sources and evidence, we make decisions about the beliefs we hold and sometimes decide that we wish to examine a given belief further. We sometimes become uncomfortable about a belief for which the evidence is clearly inadequate. But beliefs are not quickly changed, even in the face of a careful analysis that shows them to be lacking. We have become comfortable with them, and it sometimes takes years before we change them, if we ever do. A belief analysis process is thus a means for us to find out more about what we believe so that when we examine policy statements put out by our agency, when we explore the teaching approach of a part-time instructor, or when we contemplate a statement about the future direction of our program area, we will at least know more about the belief that influences what we do.

As we do an analysis, as we raise probing questions, search for presuppositions, examine definitions, and carry out the many other activities associated with analysis, we will discover an interaction: Not only do our beliefs influence how we analyze, but the process of analysis influences what we believe.

A Framework for Analyzing Continuing Education

The remainder of this book is concerned with a particular approach for analyzing continuing education practice. Five aspects of continuing education are considered: adults as learners, aims for continuing education, adult learning and teaching approaches for adults, issues involving content for continuing education, and policy and policy direction for continuing education. Chapters Five through Nine consider each of these aspects in turn.

Each of these aspects can be analyzed following three interrelated analytic approaches: critical analysis, synoptic analysis, and normative analysis. For example, one can analyze aims for continuing education from critical, synoptic, and normative perspectives. Chapters Three and Four describe in detail these three approaches to analysis.

The relationship of the five aspects of continuing education to the three approaches to analysis can be illustrated as in Table 1.

Table 1. Framework for Analyzing Continuing Education.

Aspects of Continuing Education	Analytic Approaches		
	Critical	Synoptic	Normative
Adults as learners			
Aims of continuing education			
Teaching /learning			
Content of continuing education			
Policy direction			

Overlapping Categories. There is always danger in constructing a framework with lines separating the various categories. The reality of this framework is that the lines do not exist in practice; they are placed in the framework for the purposes of understanding. For example, both synoptic and normative analysis depend on critical analysis for information. While doing speculation, as a part of the synoptic analysis, one will find it difficult to avoid the normative dimension. It thus should be obvious that the three approaches to analysis are entwined with one another.

Likewise, the dimensions of continuing education are integrally related. It makes no sense to speculate about the aims of continuing education without considering the adult learner. And sometimes the speculations about aims take the form of policy statements. It is difficult to say much about content without considering aims. The framework gives us a basis for analysis; we must always be careful when consulting frameworks that we not make more of them than intended. As we work through succeeding chapters in this book, it will become more clear that the framework is only a beginning place to guide an analysis of our practice.

Some would suggest that doing an analysis is a straightforward process with steps that can be followed. But I have discovered otherwise. Rather than a series of steps for analysis (a linear approach), I have learned the value of a spiraling approach.

A Spiraling Approach. Most of us in Western societies have learned to think linearly—that is, to follow a straight line beginning with point one, moving to point two, and continuing from point to point.

When analyzing practice from a philosophical perspective (which I am advocating), it makes more sense to pursue the process in a spiral fashion. Let me explain by illustrating from my own work. I began examining continuing education from a philosophical perspective about twenty years ago. At that time I looked generally at the field, started asking questions, and explored where philosophy fit within the field. I was trying to examine the field of continuing education comprehensively but with only minimal depth, as I reflect back on those activities. As the years passed, my interest in analyzing continuing education continued, except that, rather than dwell on the same ideas at the same level, I attempted to look at them more deeply. I considered the same ideas—the nature of the adult as learner, the purposes of continuing education, the nature of content in continuing education, and teaching and learning in continuing education. In spiral fashion, I kept coming back to the same ideas, but each time around I examined them in greater depth.

I continue with the same spiral approach in this book. I am still considering the same basic ideas that I considered twenty years ago but today in far more depth than I was able to do then. Two or three years ago I became acquainted with José Ortega y Gasset's (1960) work, which helped me understand more fully the spiraling process I had been following but had never fully understood. Ortega y Gasset, in describing how he had planned one of his books, said, "My proposal [is] not to follow a straight line but to develop my thought in successive circles of a shortening radius, hence in a spiral curve. This allows us, indeed obliges us, to present each question first in a form which is most popular, least rigorous but most understandable, certain that we will find it treated later with more energy and more formality in a narrower circle" (1960, p. 71). This book is written in this fashion—ideas are introduced in these early chapters and then explored in more depth in succeeding chapters.

I would suggest that most of us who attempt to do a systematic analysis of our practice are more apt to follow a spiral pattern than a straight-line one. Because my scientific training had taught me to pursue the answers to questions in a systematic, linear manner, it took me several years to accept as legitimate the spiral approach I was actually following. One of the great advantages of the spiral approach is its emphasis on considering many elements of the field of continuing education in context. Straight-line thinking is often reductionistic; that is, we pursue one line of thinking in great depth but at the exclusion of other lines of inquiry.

When we examine the field of continuing education, it is important to keep in context what we are doing. That is, if we are exploring some question about what direction we should take with our programming, we must also have in view those who will participate, what teaching/learning approaches will be followed, and what content will be considered. All the segments interact with one another.

Summary

Several activities can assist us as we do an analysis of our practice. These include reading; participation in the arts; creative, critical, and problem-solving thinking; writing down ideas; discussing positions with colleagues; and applying the results of one's philosophizing to one's work setting. Such application often results in new questions, and the cycle repeats.

Reflecting on one's personal beliefs is also an essential activity when analyzing continuing education. A belief analysis process includes identifying beliefs held about continuing education, searching for contradictions among beliefs, and discovering sources of beliefs and making judgments about the beliefs we hold.

A framework for analyzing continuing education includes the dimensions of adults as learners, aims, teaching/learning, content, and policy direction, as well as three approaches to analysis: critical, synoptic, and normative.

3

Conducting a Critical Examination of Practices

~~~~~~

Let us begin to look in more detail at how we might analyze our continuing education practice, starting with what I call "critical analysis." When we do a critical analysis of our continuing education practice, we examine the language we use in policy statements, in publicity material, and in the reports we write. We particularly look for slogans and metaphors, and we examine our definitions. In addition, we search for the logic or the lack of it in the written documents that relate to our day-to-day work. We also search for assumptions that undergird our practice. We may ask, what does our way of promoting a continuing education program tell us about our assumptions concerning the nature of adults as learners? When we do a critical analysis of our practice, we concentrate on dissecting what we do, and we examine the various pieces in considerable detail.

There are several specific approaches we can follow when doing a critical analysis of our practice. We can focus on one, two, or several of these approaches. Let us start with identifying assumptions.

Identifying Assumptions

Identifying assumptions differs from analytic activities discussed in this chapter that depend solely on language in that we can do it by observing practice. Of course, we can also identify assumptions by reading accounts of activities, policy statements, program plans, and other documents that describe continuing education activity.

The five dimensions of continuing education (adults as learners, aims for continuing education, teaching/learning, content for continuing education, and policy direction) can serve as guides as we attempt to identify assumptions. For instance, as we observe an adult basic education instructor teaching reading, we take account of the various instructional approaches she uses, we notice how she relates to the participants in the class, we examine the written and other classroom materials she uses, and so on. Then we ask, on the basis of what we have observed, what assumptions does this instructor hold toward adults as learners, toward teaching/learning, and so forth? Granted, we must be cautious in going very far with this analysis on the basis of only limited observation. But if we were able to observe the instructor over time and to discuss her teaching practices, use of materials, and purposes with her, we would be able to put together a reasonable list of assumptions that guided this educator's practice. We would be able to state assumptions about how she viewed teaching, how she viewed the place of content, what she believed about adults as learners, and her views on purposes.

An interesting result of doing such an analysis of practice, whether it be our own practice or that of someone else, is the often discovered contradictions between the assumptions practice suggests and the assumptions the person says he or she holds. For instance, we may espouse the importance of interactive learning, of listening carefully to the learners in our classes and workshops, and of incorporating the comments of these participants into the discussion. Yet, when we reflect on our practice or when someone else observes us and comments on what we do, we may dominate and allow little opportunity for interaction. We may not be aware of this contradiction. And when faced with the contradiction, we often do some soul searching about whether we wish to change our assumptions or our practice. However, we may be well aware of the contradictions between the assumptions we hold and our practice, and we may point out to the observer that at this particular time it was necessary to follow practice that seemed to contradict the assumptions. As those of us who have worked in the field for some time know, we need to make adjustments, we need to be flexible, and what may appear as a contradiction at one moment is not a contradiction when the entire learning experience is observed.

Another approach to identifying assumptions is to read policy statements, reports, and the like. Sometimes the assumptions are stated explicitly, but most times they are not. Let us examine some excerpts from contemporary adult education literature and see what assumptions we might identify. We will start with a quotation from a book about marketing: "If the amateurs, professionals, or in-between practitioners in continuing education publicity will follow the time frames and checklists in this book, they will find it to be a specific, exact, and logical guide to carrying out promotion and publicity on a project from its earliest beginnings through its postperformance evaluations" (Farlow, 1979, p. 4).

Without making any judgments about whether we agree or disagree with the assumptions, let us identify some.

1. Those who do continuing education can be placed into various categories—professionals, amateurs, and in-between practitioners.
2. It is necessary to promote continuing education activity.
3. Promotion includes use of time frames, checklists, and specific procedures to follow.
4. Promotion is a logical activity.
5. Adult/continuing education activities have a beginning and an end.

Upon reflecting on these assumptions, one might say that several are obvious and stating them adds little to an understanding of the paragraph quoted. To be more specific, assumptions 1, 3, and 5 are explicit assumptions. They are explicit because they are clearly expressed within the passage itself. In contrast, assumptions 2 and 4 are implicit assumptions. They are not specifically stated in the passage and may not be immediately apparent on reading the passage.

As one might expect, implicit assumptions can be controversial. One could ask, "How do you know the author of a given passage holds these implicit assumptions?" The quick answer is, one cannot be certain, but the use of words, the logic of the argument, and the examples used are indicators of implicit assumptions.

Often the implicit assumptions we identify are the most useful in gaining new perspectives about our continuing education practice. By identifying implicit assumptions, we may at times discover assumptions about our work we did not know we held. Implicit assumptions can be unconsciously presupposed. They can be so much a part of our world view, or personal perspective, that we are unaware of an alternative to them. For instance, to return to the passage quoted, if our entire experience in continuing education has always included systematic promotion of our programs, we would probably not think to write the assumption "Promotion is a logical activity." If our promotional activities have always been systematic (logical), our perspective does not include promotion that is not systematic.

Once we have identified assumptions, we can begin asking questions about them.

1. Is promotion always necessary when we do continuing education?
2. Are there approaches to promotion which differ from those coming from the business world and which fit continuing education more specifically?
3. Do we create a negative image of the purpose and worth of continuing education when we stress promotion?
4. Is it always possible, in a reductionistic fashion, to look at particular steps and procedures in carrying out an activity

such as promotion? Are there times when some broader approach to promotion may be more appropriate than a step-by-step approach?

Let us examine another quotation: "Now a new note is appearing in American educational thought: adults *must* continue to learn; learning, like breathing, is a requirement of living. The assumption that learning is a lifelong process is based on a new fact of life: the accelerating pace of social change. For the first time in the history of civilization, the time span of drastic cultural change has been telescoped into less than the lifetime of the individual. The current generation of mature adults now represents the first generation faced with managing a culture different *in kind* than the one originally transmitted to them. The consequence of this new fact of life is such that the well-educated youth of today is an obsolete man tomorrow" (Jensen, Liveright, and Hallenbeck, 1964, p. iv).

Assumptions we might derive from this paragraph include the following:

1. Many adults have not continued to learn throughout their lifetime.
2. Cultural change in the 1960s was more drastic than at other times in the history of humankind.
3. Learning is more crucial now than it has been in the past.
4. What one has learned as a youth may not be relevant when one becomes an adult.
5. People seek to manage their culture.
6. Learning will contribute to managing culture.
7. It is possible for everyone to learn, no matter the age.
8. All persons must continue to learn throughout their lifetime, or something "drastic" is likely to occur.
9. Individuals can make a difference in managing culture.

As we reflect on these assumptions, we can ask many questions:

1. Is it conceivable that anyone living can stop learning? Does not basic survival require learning?

2. How does the author define learning? Is it something that one can do by oneself? How does learning relate to education and educators?

3. What is the relationship between learning and "managing culture"? Are there other factors as important as what one has learned, such as political and economic considerations? Does it matter what we have learned if the predominant political ideology at the time advocates a particular approach to cultural change? Can we as individuals do very much in managing culture, or is such "managing" accomplished through group activity?

4. Will people not learn naturally without someone reminding them of the importance of learning?

5. Was the cultural change described by the authors any more drastic than those faced by societies over the centuries?

6. Might cultural change not be so dynamic and complex that much of it occurs by chance and can never be managed, no matter how much people learn or how many people learn and are involved?

Identifying assumptions is an interesting, not difficult activity that often results in new insights about practice, policy statements, and other written materials in continuing education. Often what is not said but implied is more valuable than what is said. With careful listening, reading, and reflection, we can identify assumptions and then begin to ask questions that help us understand more deeply the meaning of practice and of various written materials.

Clarifying Definitions

When we read a policy statement developed by someone in our agency or institution, when we read a promotional brochure describing a new adult education program, when we write a report of our activities over the past twelve months, we confront definitions. Are they accurate and do they convey what is intended? Or do they take too much for granted—that is, does the writer of the definition have one thing in mind while the reader perceives something quite different?

Definitions have been a problem in continuing education for a long time. On the one hand, there is considerable diversity —we have several definitions for the same thing and often cannot agree. On the other hand, many of our definitions are vague and do not communicate what is intended.

For instance, we have much difficulty defining the word *adult*. We all seem to know what the term means, at least at one level, for we are all adults. But when we write policy statements, when we write grant proposals, and when we write curricula for continuing education activities of various kinds, we are faced with defining the term. Some do it simply, or so they think, by defining an adult as anyone over age eighteen. As an arbitrary, rather precise definition that places people into categories, the definition works. From a practical perspective, it poses many questions. Why is someone who is just short of eighteen years not an adult? What about the person who is twenty-five years of age but acts as if he or she were seventeen, and so on? We have all heard the rebuttals to using age as a way of defining *adult*. We then go on and try to define *adult* as "someone who is mature." And we again find ourselves in difficulty, for as soon as we use a word like *mature* we must then define it as well, and we seem to dig ourselves deeper and deeper into our definitional morass.

Israel Scheffler (1960, pp. 11-35) offers some insight into understanding definitions and evaluating them. He says that we in education use essentially four types of definitions: scientific, stipulative, descriptive, and programmatic.

Scientific Definitions. Scientific definitions are those that come out of scientific research. An example would be a definition of *adult* described in terms of the cessation of certain bone growth. This definition is derived from scientific theory and evidence and thus must be considered within the theoretical context in which it was developed.

Stipulative Definitions. Stipulative definitions, according to Scheffler, present a word or cluster of words declared equivalent to some other word or symbols. For example, if we were writing a curriculum with subsections designed for particular groups of adults, we could call the first group of adults group A, the second group B, and so on. We have defined the groups by the letters assigned to them. When we later referred to group A or group B, our reader would know to which group we were referring.

Another example of a stipulative definition is the definition that adults are those who are eighteen years of age and older. We may argue with a stipulative definition, but we are usually able to understand what this type of definition is communicating.

Descriptive Definitions. Descriptive definitions go further than stipulative definitions. Descriptive definitions portray various aspects of a phenomenon and often draw from several sources in assisting the reader to understand the phenomenon. For instance, we can define the adult as learner from a psychological perspective, from a sociological perspective, from a historical perspective, and so on.

When we evaluate a descriptive definition, we look to see whether the words used reflect what Scheffler calls "normal predefinitional usage." If, for example, a definition of *adult learning* included the words *behavioral growth,* we could legitimately question the definition. The words *behavioral* and *growth* are not ordinarily placed together. As those familiar with the literature of adult learning will attest, *behavioral* refers to one broad definition of *learning* while *growth* refers to a quite different one.

Sometimes, though, we use ordinary words, those that have agreed-on definitions, in new ways. We do this to attract attention to a new set of ideas. We do it to encourage a reader to view a situation in a new way. The danger in giving a new definition to a word commonly used is the confusion it creates in understanding. For instance, suppose we say that "adult learners are fragile." In this case we need to say more to communicate what we mean. The word *fragile* ordinarily means "breaking easily." When we say that adult learners are fragile, we may mean that they are sensitive to our words and actions and easily influenced by them.

We, of course, often use metaphors to assist our understanding of various phenomena within continuing education.

The word *growth*, used to describe adult learning, is a metaphor
that comes out of agriculture and the planting and nurturing of
crops. I will say more about metaphors later in this chapter.

Programmatic Definitions. Programmatic definitions indicate what should be done—they state a direction for activity.
For instance, if we say that education of adults is for developing
learners who can learn on their own with little outside assistance, we have written a programmatic definition. Whereas descriptive definitions attempt to explain and assist our understanding of something, programmatic definitions go further.
They tell us what we ought to be doing or what results we
might expect.

In summary, what are some practical applications of clarifying definitions? Do a critical analysis of a policy statement, a
curriculum plan, or a statement of an organization's long-range
goals and objectives. Look for how the terms are defined. Some
of the questions to ask are (1) Do I clearly understand the
meanings of the words used? For instance, if the writer is talking about growth as an outcome of an educational program, has
the writer said enough so that I understand what he or she
means by *growth*? (2) Is the writer conventional in the use of
words; that is, are the words used the way they are commonly
defined in our everyday use of them? If not has the writer gone
on to explain the new use? The final, more global questions to
ask are: Do I believe the writer knows clearly and precisely
what he or she is saying, and do I understand the definitions in
the same way that I believe the writer understands them?

Searching for Metaphors

In the simplest sense, a metaphor comes from giving a
name to something that belongs to something else. When we
say, "That institution is a sleeping giant," we are giving the institution a name that belongs to something else. "Metaphor is
a way of knowing—one of the oldest, most deeply embedded,
even indispensable ways of knowing in the history of human
consciousness. It is, at its simplest, a way of proceeding from

the known to the unknown. It is a way of cognition in which the identifying qualities of one thing are transferred in an instantaneous, almost unconscious flash of insight to some other thing that is, by remoteness or complexity, unknown to us" (Nisbet, 1969, p. 4).

Single words, sentences, or paragraphs may be used as metaphors. Sometimes the tone of a piece of writing, which is evoked by how words are used, can be a metaphor. As Scheffler points out, "We may regard the metaphorical statement as indicating that there is an important analogy between two things, without saying explicitly in what the analogy consists" (1960, p. 48). For instance, using the preceding example, we would usually not explain that the reason we called the institution a sleeping giant was that it had characteristics similar to those of sleeping giants. We use metaphors because of their power in evoking meaning and feeling without explicit explanation. Metaphors can be extremely powerful because they are often subtle and because the meanings they evoke are often wrapped in vivid pictures. "Metaphor is our means of effecting instantaneous fusion of two separated realms of experience into one illuminating, iconic, encapsulating image" (Nisbet, 1969, p. 4).

Metaphors are used freely in continuing education, often without our full knowledge that we are using them. For instance, when we say we are developing a "strategic plan," we are drawing on a war metaphor, as *strategic planning* is a term from military theory and practice. We often do this without being aware of the roots of the metaphor.

In many ways, metaphoric knowledge is the opposite of knowledge that we gain from experience, from reading, from our association with people, and from research of various types. Metaphoric knowledge leaps beyond the accumulation of knowledge to an "aha" type of knowledge. Metaphoric knowledge, when we reflect on it, is more similar to that knowledge we call insight. Insight comes when we least expect it and often puts together ideas in ways we had not anticipated. Metaphoric knowledge does that as well.

But as pointed out earlier, we are not always aware of the metaphoric knowledge we have and use, and consequently in some ways metaphoric knowledge can communicate what is not intended. For example, if we disagree that continuing education should be compared to the military, and yet we freely use words such as *strategy, fighting the good fight,* or *doing battle,* we are communicating a war metaphor. We do this without knowing we are doing it, often because our colleagues, supervisors, and policy makers are doing it. And they too often use the words without being aware.

Some metaphors change over time. For instance, a hundred years ago educators talked about the human brain as having an intricate network of roadways, some well traveled and familiar, others new and unexplored. A generation or so later, educators talked about the brain's complex "telephone organization" in which messages were sent over neuron "wires" to all parts of the body. Today we read about the brain as a computer with the ability to store, retain, and call up information. Other metaphors do not change. We can still read about "putting the cart before the horse" and keeping our "nose to the grindstone," although we find few carts before or after horses and have to search in a museum for a grindstone.

What are some common metaphors used in continuing education? In succeeding chapters we will explore metaphors relating directly to adults as learners, to teaching and learning, to content, and to aims for the field and their use in policy statements. But for now, let us examine one rather common metaphor used in continuing education and see how it is expressed. The metaphor is continuing education as a factory. Seldom will we see the metaphor expressed directly—"Continuing education is like a factory." What we do find is an assortment of words and phrases that have their roots in descriptions of factories and factory functions. We talk about inputs and outputs. So many hours of instruction will "yield" these skills and this knowledge gained. We do a "cost/benefit analysis," and we ask whether it is "economical" to hold a class for X number of students given an "overhead" cost of Y, an instructor cost of Z, and the need for P amount of "profit." When something goes wrong with our plans, we sometimes hear that someone has "put sand in the gears." An instructor who is deemed out of date is encouraged to "re-tool" so he or she can be "productive" again. As we examine how we might improve what we are doing, we sometimes talk about an "efficiency analysis." We occasionally talk about those who complete our programs as the "products" of our efforts.

Whether we intend to or not, we use many words and phrases from the factory metaphor. When we do that and when we reflect on the words we have used, we conclude that we are communicating that continuing education is like a factory.

This realization leads us to the point of making judgments. Do we agree with the metaphors we use? Do we agree with the metaphors others in our field use? When focusing on metaphors, we first become aware of those being used. We next ask, what is it we wish to communicate? Which metaphors do that well, and which are the antithesis of what we believe should be communicated?

When we criticize metaphors, some can be dismissed because they are either trivial or too vague to communicate understanding and feeling. For instance, we might read that adult learners are like oak trees. They may be, but it is not clear without saying more about the oak tree that the tree will serve as an appropriate metaphor. Scheffler (1960) notes that we can also criticize metaphors by examining where the analogies they indicate break down. "Every metaphor is limited in this way, giving only a certain perspective on its subject, which may be supplemented by other perspectives" (p. 48).

Scheffler says we can examine metaphors in the same way we examine theories of something. A given theory may help us understand one perspective of something; another theory may help us understand a different perspective. Likewise, a given metaphor may help us understand one aspect of continuing education, and another metaphor may help us understand another aspect. "A comparison of alternative metaphors may be as illuminating as a comparison of alternative theories, in indicating the many-faceted character of a subject. Such a comparison may also provide a fresh sense of the uniqueness of the subject, for to know in what ways something is like many different things is to know a good deal about what makes it distinctive, different from each" (pp. 48-49).

Examining Slogans

We use slogans often in continuing education. "Start where the learner is," "We are learner-oriented, not content-oriented," "Our programs are based on learners' needs," and "Andragogy, not pedagogy" are examples. "Slogans in education provide rallying symbols of the key ideas and attitudes of educational movements. They both express and foster community of spirit, attracting new adherents and providing reassurance and strength to veterans. They are thus analogous to religious and political slogans and, like these, products of the party spirit" (Scheffler, 1960, p. 36).

Slogans are coined for a variety of reasons. One major reason, as the statement just quoted points out, is for people to rally around a new idea or movement. Because continuing education as we know it today is relatively new, several slogans were developed as rallying phrases. Perhaps the most noted of these, particularly during the past ten to fifteen years, has been "Andragogy, not pedagogy." Knowles (1980) made the case that the education of adults should be different from the education of children for several reasons relating to maturity, reasons for learning, and life experience. He referred to this "new" education for adults as andragogy, a term he borrowed from Europe, and contrasted it with pedagogy, the educational practice followed for the education of children. Within ten years the term *andragogy* had entered the literature of continuing education. It became a term used in speeches about the practice of educating adults. It was used in the promotion literature for workshops, conferences, and graduate programs catering to adults. It has even been used to describe the kind of person desired to fill empty staff positions—"We want a person who knows how to practice andragogy."

Dušan Savićević, Professor of Andragogy, University of Belgrade, Yugoslavia, says *andragogy* as used in the United States is far more narrowly defined than it is in several European countries (personal communication, 1984). Savićević explains that in Yugoslavia and some other countries, such as Hungary, Poland, and Germany, andragogy is the theory of adult/continuing education. *Andragogy* does not refer to a technology of teaching adults, a commonly used definition in this country. Rather, andragogy examines the meanings of terminology, the place for andragogy in the system of scientific disciplines, the problems of classifying andragogical disciplines, the relation of andragogy to pedagogy, and the relation of andragogy to other social sciences such as sociology, economics, and psychology. Savićević points out that the word can be traced back to at least 1833, when the German teacher Alexander Kapp used it. At the turn of the century, Ludo Hartmann, founder of the People's University of Vienna, used the term, and in the 1920s Eduard Lindeman, an American adult educator, used it (Lindeman, [1926] 1961, p. 1).

Other, older slogans continue to be popular in the field. We still hear "We focus on learning by doing," "We educate for action," and "We teach adults, not subject matter."

There is, of course, a place for slogans in continuing education. Slogans often emerge as a response to inadequate practice. Knowles emphasized andragogy as a response to what he perceived as inadequate practice—educators of adults were following youth education principles when conducting educational programs for adults. A danger with slogans, though, is that they sometimes persist and refer to a situation that is no longer present, or they mask rather than clarify a situation. For instance, many elementary and secondary educators and administrators would argue that the pedagogy that Knowles discusses is no longer present in classrooms. They make the point that much of the youth education of today has characteristics similar to andragogy, and so the rallying cry for andragogy, not pedagogy, makes little sense today. (That is not to say that young people and adults are viewed as the same and that all educational practice should be conducted in an identical fashion no matter what the age or experience of the participants.)

Some slogans, when examined literally, make no sense, yet they can be valuable nevertheless. The slogan "We teach adults, not subject matter" is an example. If we tried to follow that slogan literally, and someone asked us what we teach, we would reply, "We teach adults." The questioner would likely look at us a bit strangely and ask, "But what do you teach them?" And our reply would be, if we followed the slogan literally, "We do not teach them anything." That, of course, would not be true; we indeed do teach them something, even if our teaching is an attempt to help them become aware of something they already know. If we teach adults, we must be teaching something—there must be some content involved, some topic, some question, some attitude or feeling, something. If there is nothing, it would appear that our teaching then is not teaching.

The point is that, if pressed, we would concede that we indeed do teach something, so that the slogan "We teach adults, not subject matter" is literally incorrect. But we may still find the slogan useful, for although it takes an impossibly extreme position, it nevertheless focuses attention on those educators of adults who stress subject matter at the expense of the adult learner. The slogan helps us understand an attitude toward the education of adults that emphasizes the learner.

Slogans are also used as rallying points for competing educational theories. For instance, the slogan "Our program is competency-based" comes out of a behavioral change theory of learning, in which outcomes (competencies) are identified and the educator teaches for the competency. A contrasting slogan is "Education for growth," which comes from a Gestalt field theory of learning, in which the emphasis is not on competencies to be learned but on understanding broad concepts and long-range views.

Some slogans have metaphors embedded in them. For example, the slogan popular in the cooperative extension at this writing, "We plan for impact," has the metaphor "impact" in it. Hence, when we do an analysis of this slogan, we must also reflect on the meaning and the root of the metaphor "impact." (*Impact* comes from the world of heavy industry, where one object hits another and changes it in some way—crushes it, molds it, modifies its form.)

Slogans sometimes follow the vogue words of the day. "Our adult education program is results-oriented" is an example. "Results-oriented" is a vogue buzzword popular at this writing. Or we may hear "We plan for alternative scenarios," "We are mobilizing our resources," and "The bottom line of our agency is training for jobs." Five years from now we will likely have replaced "scenario," "mobilizing our resources," and "bottom line" with some equally catchy buzz phrases that come out of the government or business or the military, or maybe we will invent a few ourselves.

How do we go about evaluating and making judgments about the slogans used in our field? I have already given some examples. One question to ask is, What situation caused the slogan to emerge, and does that situation still exist today? That is, is the slogan still appropriate today? Recall the example of andragogy and pedagogy. Another tack is to examine the slogan to see whether metaphors are embedded in it and whether it contains vogue buzzwords. In the previous section I suggested some approaches for examining metaphors. Vogue buzzwords are often problems when used in slogans. Everyone thinks he or she knows what vogue buzzwords mean and tosses them around indiscriminately. They are used so much, in so many situations, often inappropriately, that we all tire of them and they die a merciful death. Unfortunately, new vogue buzzwords are waiting to replace the old ones, and we quickly embed them in our slogans.

Slogans sometimes take on the characteristics of definitions. "With the passage of time . . . slogans are often increasingly interpreted more literally both by adherents and by critics of the movements they represent. They are taken more and more as literal doctrines or arguments, rather than merely as rallying symbols. When this happens in a given case, it becomes important to evaluate the slogan both as a straightforward assertion and as a symbol of a practical social movement, without, moreover, confusing the one with the other" (Scheffler, 1960, pp. 36-37). For example, andragogy has, for some educators of adults, become a definition for the field, a set of guidelines for practice. Andragogy has thus become, for some, more than a slogan and therefore must be examined as a definition would be examined.

Raising Questions

An important activity in critical analysis is raising questions. In an attempt to clarify our own practice or clarify the activities of others, we ask particular kinds of questions: (1) those that relate to clarifying concepts and (2) those that come out of metaphysics, epistemology, or axiology.

Questions About Concepts. Elias and Merriam (1980, pp. 183-184), drawing on the literature of analytic philosophy, discuss questions of concept that "entail examining ways in which such words as *democracy* and *communism* are used. Analysis involves making a cognitive map of the ways in which the two concepts are used in order to see the similarities and dissimilarities between the terms. Another way of phrasing a question of concept is to ask whether the one can exist without the other. ... Questions of concept are answered not by merely giving definitions of the terms but by examining the ways in which the terms are used. We can adequately analyze concepts by comparing and contrasting them to concepts [to] which they are similar."

For example, the concept "program" is used often in continuing education. We can ask questions about how the concept "program" relates to the concept of curriculum. We can also ask how "program" relates to activity or event. By doing so, we can begin to see the variety of ways that the concept of program is used in the field and to understand more fully the meaning of the various uses. Sometimes we use "program" to mean a carefully planned set of offerings with a structured content (relating to *curriculum* as the term is often used in formal education). At other times we use "program" to mean a single event such as an evening workshop or an interview conducted on television.

Conceptual analysts, as Elias and Merriam point out, use the technique of identifying *model cases* and *contrary cases* to clarify concepts. Model cases are examples that people agree are good uses of the concept. For example, although "program" may have several definitions, educators of adults might generally agree that a several-session noncredit course is a good use of the concept, as is what an agency or institution plans to accomplish over the period of a year. Although these two uses of "program" are different, educators of adults might agree that these are good and proper uses of the concept. In contrast, when someone calls an isolated slide show, a single presentation, an "adult education program," this use may be questioned and is presented as a contrary case. When suggesting the use of model and contrary cases, we are following the simple procedure of relating what something is to something like it and what something is to something it is clearly not.

Questions from Metaphysics, Epistemology, and Axiology. When we analyze our practice drawing on philosophy, we can be guided by questions that the disciplines of metaphysics, epistemology, and axiology suggest.

Metaphysics is concerned with questions about reality. Examples include: What is the nature of human nature, and what is the essence of adulthood? Philosophers, when examining metaphysical questions, often reflect on opposing positions. Some of the classic opposing positions are mind versus matter, structure versus function, harmony versus conflict, action versus reflection, free will versus determinism, certainty versus uncertainty, and reality versus appearances (Moore, 1979, p. 20).

For instance, in continuing education we may ask, do adult learners have free will or is what adults do essentially determined? Or we could inquire, is an adult learner's perception of what he or she needs more reasonable as a basis for programming than what a review of statistical information suggests are needs of adult learners? Many more such questions relate to these and other dichotomies.

As explained earlier, when we ask metaphysical questions, we are searching for fundamentals. We want to go beneath the surface and look more deeply. We are not satisfied, for example, with descriptive information about who participates in our programs, such as age, occupation, and reasons for participating. We are not satisfied with psychological and sociological information about our participants. That is not to say that we lack interest in descriptive, psychological, and sociological information, but we want to go further to examine and reflect on questions about free will, whether human beings are fundamentally active or passive by nature, and whether a search for meaning is an inherent characteristic of the human condition.

Answers to these fundamental questions may help us as

practitioners understand in greater depth such matters as what teaching approaches are most effective when working with adult audiences. If we believe that adults are by nature active and that all adults, to some degree, are searching for meaning in their lives, then we will plan teaching approaches accordingly. Our teaching will allow for interaction between teacher and learners and among learners, it will allow for learners to solve practical problems they have encountered in their work and in their lives, and it will encourage learners to help plan their learning activities. Moreover, in many instances, we will encourage self-directed learning in which we as instructors will have little involvement. Our teaching will also encourage time for reflection on what was taught and questions that generate thinking about the meaning of the educational experience. Too often, in our haste to "cover the material," insufficient attention is given to exploring meaning.

Epistemology is concerned with knowledge. What is knowledge, and how do we come to know something? For those of us in education, questions related to epistemology take on special importance. Knowledge and coming to know imply learning. Therefore questions of epistemology are often at the core of what we do in continuing education.

The question "What is knowledge?" can be answered in a variety of ways. Moore (1979, p. 23) writes, "Knowledge is often referred to as: (1) facts or factual information, (2) ideas, concepts, insights . . . concerning something, (3) understandings of relationships and principles, (4) mindful behavior patterns, (5) skills or the how-to-do something intelligently, (6) memorizations in meaningful ways, (7) conscious choice, (8) prediction with high degree of probability, (9) comprehension of data observed, (10) awareness of things and concepts in relationships, (11) mathematical analogy and its use, (12) verification of theory in practice."

Of course, not everyone would accept each of these as "knowledge." For instance, some would argue that facts or information are not knowledge until the individual who has accumulated them makes sense out of them by putting them into his or her personal perspective. Facts and information remain so until they are examined by the receiver, and not until they have been worked on do they become knowledge.

Another question often asked is, what are the sources of knowledge? And which sources of knowledge are we willing to accept and which will we reject? The literature of philosophy generally refers to four broad knowledge sources: sensory impressions, rational thought, authorities, and intuition.

Knowledge from sensory impressions is that knowledge we gain from seeing, hearing, smelling—what we gain from direct sensory experience. Questions we might explore are, can we always trust our senses? Is what we obtain through our senses consistent with the reality of what is being seen, heard, and so forth? In other words, is there a difference between what is perceived and the reality of the situation? Or do we wish to define reality as that which is perceived and deny the existence of an ultimate reality? Are we willing to accept knowledge that ultimately comes from a source other than sensory experience?

When one sits down and tries to logically think through a problem or reflects about the relationship of ideas or attempts to combine ideas, facts, and information into some type of logical order, the results can be called knowledge from rational thought. Questions can be raised. Is the knowledge that results from this process really new knowledge or simply putting together existing knowledge? Others might argue that putting together existing knowledge in new ways indeed produces new knowledge, often more "important" knowledge than the sources that were combined. Are the results for logical thought followed? And a rebuttal argument is, what difference does it make whether formal rules for logic were followed, if new, important, and worthwhile knowledge resulted?

In many applied fields, including continuing education, much attention is paid to authorities. We cite the writings of Ralph Tyler, John Dewey, Carl Rogers, Cyril Houle, Eduard Lindeman, Malcolm Knowles, and a host of others. What they say becomes a source of knowledge for us. Many questions can be raised about knowledge from authorities. Is this particular authority dependable? Can we trust the information he or she is providing us? What criteria will we use to sort out the accurate from the inaccurate knowledge, the applicable from the inapplicable, when we look to authorities for knowledge? Is the experience from which a particular authority developed the information we are abstracting sufficiently similar to our experience that it makes sense to use it? Are we developing dependency relationships when we put too much emphasis on knowledge from authorities and too little on our ability to generate knowledge?

Of the four sources of knowledge, knowledge from intuition is the most controversial. Bruyn (1966, p. 167) describes intuition as "that knowledge which is derived from the feelings, sentiments, and manifest human spirit which has acquired some measure of independence from the senses and the logical powers of man. *As we conceive it, intuition is the capacity to apprehend personal meanings* which inhere in a social context. It is a human capacity which, like logic or sense, can be disciplined, and a set of procedures may be developed around it for purposes of gaining knowledgeable access to this portion of man's nature." Again we can ask questions. Is knowledge from intuition (usually called insight) dependable? Or is it so individualized that any value it might have would accrue only to the person who had the insight? Should knowledge from intuition be considered knowledge, especially in light of the difficulty in really explaining its source? Most persons who experience an insight cannot explain where it came from or what procedures they followed in arriving at the insight. Hence another person seldom has the opportunity to arrive at the same insight.

What are the relationships among these four sources of knowledge, if we are willing to accept them as sources? Are some more important than others? Should some precede others as we try to obtain knowledge? That is, should we first go to an authority, then to our own personal senses? Should our choice of knowledge sources depend on what we are trying to find out about something?

Axiology, the third branch of philosophy from which questions arise, is concerned with ethics and esthetics. Ethics is concerned with right and wrong, good and bad, desirable and undesirable. Esthetics is concerned with beauty and nonbeauty, in artistic creation and in everyday human life. Thus axiology is concerned with questions of value. Examples include: What is the relationship of the educator's values to the participant's values? Which individuals or groups should be the primary concern for continuing education programs? What should be the social responsibility of continuing education programs? Or we can ask axiological questions in another vein and relate them to worthwhileness of programs—questions that often become a part of evaluation and accountability activities. We could inquire about the worth of a particular program and then explore the many subquestions that result: Worth from whose point of view? An agency's perspective? The participant's? The educator's? The taxpayer's, if the program is tax-supported? Many of the questions evaluators ask have their roots in axiology.

The two major theories of values are called "objectivism" and "subjectivism" (Brauner and Burns, 1965, p. 9). Objectivism refers to values as independent of humankind, and subjectivism refers to values as dependent on humankind. Many subtheories of values exist, but all fit into these two broad theories. Those who subscribe to objectivist value theories believe that values exist "out there" and that we need to discover what they are. Those subscribing to subjectivist theories of values believe that we as human beings develop values and that values cannot exist independent of humanity.

> Some philosophers defend the idea that we can only *create* values, or opinions about them, for ourselves and that we can have no rational justification for thinking that any of them apply to everyone [subjectivism]. Others hold that certain basic values or virtues or ideals have validity for all people and only their implementation varies from one place or time to another [objectivism]. Some argue that values are applicable only to acts that relate to other people or to God; others hold in whatever circumstances people may find themselves, social or private, they should act to pursue certain values and follow certain principles of conduct. There are those who claim that different values or ideals ap-

ply to people with different backgrounds, intelligence, social class, economic status, genetic makeup, knowledge of the world. . . . Others would argue that ethical considerations apply to all human beings equally, by virtue of their being human [Machan, 1977, pp. 30-31].

It is thus easy to see that values and the study of values are extremely complex, yet that in no way diminishes their importance to us as educators of adults.

Ethics is a particular area of inquiry within axiology, with concern for morally approved or disapproved behavior. Ethics has specific application to the field of continuing education. Singarella and Sork (1983, p. 246) raise these questions: "What ethical skills are used daily in the adult educator's contract (implied or written) with clients? What is the responsibility of professional training programs to deal with ethics in preparing future adult educators? Is an ethical code for adult education feasible or desirable? What happens when personal ethical codes conflict with those of administrative superiors?"

Although the field of continuing education has not developed a set of ethical guidelines or an ethical code, the question of what is ethical behavior for an educator of adults cannot be avoided. Ethical behavior is, of course, based on our values, and as the questions just raised imply, people's values are not all the same. Thus what one person accepts as ethical behavior may be viewed as unethical by another. An important question to ask, then, as educators of adults, is whether there are fundamental values that transcend a society and do not vary from person to person (although some less fundamental values may vary) and thus whether there are ethical behaviors that should be identified and accepted as appropriate. Many would argue that there are such fundamental values and therefore that it is possible to identify what is and what is not ethical behavior. To examine this question in the most fundamental way, we could ask what our position is on the value of human life. If we would agree that we hold highly the value of human life as a fundamental value, then we can begin to examine our activities that touch people's lives, to see whether we are consistent with that basic value in what we do as educators. Do our teaching approaches complement our concern for the well-being of our participants? Do our program development efforts emphasize, in a fundamental way, our concern for people and their well-being? Are we more concerned about our participants than about the survival of our agency or institution, and so on?

Esthetics, the second component of axiology, is concerned with questions of beauty and art. We often define esthetics solely as an appreciation or creation of the arts, failing to recognize that esthetics has much broader application. If we, as educators of adults, develop a broad feeling for esthetics that goes beyond the arts to nearly every aspect of what we do as educators, we will ask questions with esthetic roots. But first we may need to explore and develop an appreciation of esthetics as an inherent characteristic of the human condition, something that all of us strive for. This appreciation has its roots in basic beliefs about human nature.

If we accept love for and appreciation of beauty as an inherent characteristic of human nature, what kinds of questions might we ask of our activities as educators of adults? Of course, obvious questions about whether participants have access to good literature, art, music, drama, and dance could be asked. But as I have suggested earlier, concern for esthetics goes much further than the arts themselves. We need to ask questions about the climate for the learning activities we plan. Are we sufficiently concerned for the facilities, for the amenities, for the "little" extra things that make programs pleasant? Are we concerned about how educational programs are organized; are the various activities blended together in such a way that learning is facilitated but also in a way that contributes to a sense of beauty in the organizational scheme? Are presenters concerned for the style of their presentations, the quality of visuals, the elegance of the organizational scheme? I am not suggesting multiprojector presentations and otherwise elaborate visual aids. Sometimes the expensive presentation lacks the elegance of something done simply but thoughtfully and carefully. Thus a concern for esthetics can and ought to pervade what we do as educators of adults. Unfortunately, we often accept that esthetics relates only to the arts and so we are not concerned with it in our everyday programming.

Examining Reasoning

Reasoning, in philosophy often called logic, is a major area of inquiry and requires far more space than can be allotted here. Moreover, when one begins exploring the literature of logic, it becomes clear that disagreement abounds, so that no universally agreed-on statement about logic and how to do it exists. In addition, if we reflect on reasoning as an approach to thinking, we must be aware of critical, creative, and problem-solving thinking—all of which can contribute to critical analysis along with logic (see Chapter Two).

Here I will touch briefly on what logic is and suggest one approach for doing "informal logic." Let us begin with a definition. Logic "is not concerned with the *reality* about which we are thinking but only with the *operation of thinking* itself" (McCall, 1952, p. xvii). Or, said another way, "Logic does not supply the materials that go into argument, nor does it make value judgments. It is a process for sound thinking, and if a conclusion turns out to be a poor one even though the requirements of logic were complied with in reaching it, then the fault was in the material or the value judgments and not in logic. . . . Logic can be pictured as a coin with two sides. One side is positive; it is concerned with the requirements for sound thinking. The other side is negative; its province is mistakes in reasoning—that is, fallacies" (Fearnside, 1980, p. 3).

Two terms used often in discussions of logic are *argument* and *fallacy*. *Argument* refers to a chain of reasoning that results in a conclusion. It does not refer to a disagreement, which is a common meaning for the term. *Fallacy* refers to a faulty argument—that is, the reasoning process was flawed in some way. *Fallacy* is not used to describe a conclusion believed false.

Thus logic is a process of thinking, or, to be more specific, a process of thinking that presents a sequence of reasoning leading to a conclusion. One might ask, what is so profound about this? Do not we all, as a part of living, reason our way to conclusions? When we decide what clothing to put on in the morning, when we decide what to eat for lunch, when we decide where we will go on vacation or what automobile we will purchase or what our position will be on nuclear warheads, we are practicing logical thought. Is not this common-sense reasoning good enough? McCall (1952) suggests, "Though common sense is a necessary prerequisite to all effective thinking, it is not sufficient by itself to insure correct procedure. . . . Common sense, unchecked by logical criticism or scientific investigation, [leads to] folklore, assuring us that the earth is fixed and the sun moves, that spirit is breath, that everything which moves is alive, and that only the palpable is real" (p. xviii).

Although McCall's comments may be a bit overdrawn, he does allow for the importance of both common sense, which he calls "natural logic," and "acquired logic," that reasoning approach which builds on natural logic. In what does "acquired logic" consist? What must we do to practice it? "We must learn to organize our concepts and our judgments and our inferences, to express them precisely, and to extract from our own thoughts and experiences, as well as from those of others as expressed in words, their complete and exact meaning. We must learn to detect beneath the flesh of rhetoric the sinews of argument. A good logician will never mistake a platitude for a principle, or a generality for a universal" (McCall, 1952, p. xx).

The classic approach to logic is the syllogism:

> Every A is B
> Every C is A
> Therefore, every C is B.

To take an overly simplistic example to make the point, assign the letters as follows: A = adults, B = learners, C = participants. Then construct the syllogism:

> Every adult is a learner
> Every participant is an adult
> Therefore, every participant is a learner.

Of course, not every argument in continuing education falls so neatly into a syllogism as that one.

What approach might we follow in analyzing an argument in continuing education, one that could be a part of a mission statement, a policy, or a report? The following, which draws on the work of Anthony Weston (1982, pp. 135-137), is suggested. The procedure is best referred to as "informal logic."

1. Is there an argument? An argument, as defined here, is a set of premises that results in a conclusion. Some statements are not arguments, for they contain facts and figures, emotional appeals, and anecdotes but reach no conclusions, or they present a conclusion but offer no defense of how the conclusion was reached.

2. What are the premises for the argument? What major ideas are offered to support the conclusion presented?

3. What is the conclusion(s)? That is, what is the main point of the argument presented?

4. What kind of argument is it? Deductive (argues from universal to particulars)? Inductive (argues from particular to general)?

5. Are supporting data sufficient? Are the data diverse to prevent or make unlikely systematic bias?

6. If a deductive argument, are counterpositions mentioned? If an inductive argument, are cases omitted that may contradict the conclusion?

7. Are common fallacies in evidence? Common fallacies include seeking to discredit the source by personal attack, appealing to tradition, use of emotive language, inconsistency, and suggesting cause and effect because one event precedes another. (See Fearnside, 1980, for a comprehensive discussion of thirty-eight common fallacies.)

8. Are the premises true? Are the factual information and other evidence presented in support of the premises accurate?

9. What is your decision about both the process used for the argument and the accuracy of the content of the argument?

Several of the phases in the "informal" logic process are controversial. A classical logician would argue that one should not mix making judgments about the accuracy of the content of the argument with making judgments about the accuracy of the procedure for the argument. The classical logician would argue that, when practicing logic, one should be concerned only for "the process of sound thinking." It seems reasonable, though, when we in continuing education wish to check our own processes for arguing a position, or when we wish to analyze someone else's argument, that we combine a concern for content and process.

McPeck (1981) argues that no standard logical procedure can be applied to an argument, because arguments vary in different fields of inquiry. He therefore emphasizes competency in a field of inquiry before an attempt is made to do a logical analysis of policy statements and other arguments. "It is not the logical validity of an argument which we find difficult, but rather determining whether certain premises are in fact true. And this latter difficulty invariably takes us into the unfamiliar ground of some technical subject area, where each question seems to generate several others, and epistemological uncertainties abound" (p. 221).

McPeck emphasizes the need to pay particular attention to not only the quantity of evidence in an argument but its quality. One must be well versed in a field of inquiry before attempting a logical analysis of its policy statements, position papers, and other documents in which argument is used.

In addition, when we try to analyze arguments in continuing education, we can often find useful the information we gained from following the procedures discussed earlier in this chapter: identifying assumptions, clarifying definitions, searching for metaphors, examining slogans, and raising questions. Information from these procedures can be particularly helpful as we do a logical analysis.

Summary

Critical analysis of continuing education practice includes identifying assumptions, clarifying definitions, searching for metaphors, examining slogans, raising questions, and examining reasoning.

Assumptions can be identified from observing practice as well as reading various written statements, including policy documents. Clarifying definitions helps us to sharpen our thinking and more clearly communicate our meaning about what we do. Identifying and questioning metaphors assists us in understanding the deeper meanings of what we say about our practice. Occasionally the meaning communicated by a metaphor we use is not the meaning we intend. Slogans can serve as rallying cries for program direction but must be examined to see whether they continue to be relevant and whether they communicate what we intend. When doing a critical analysis from a philosophical perspective, we can be guided by questions from the disciplines of metaphysics, epistemology, and axiology. We can also raise questions about such concepts as "program" and "curriculum." By examining the reasoning we use in reaching various decisions and the reasoning used in the development of various written materials, such as policy statements, we can analyze the soundness of our thinking.

Critical analysis, from a philosophical perspective, is thus concerned with examining, in considerable detail, various aspects of our practice.

4

Continuing Education in the Context of Other Fields

~~~~~~

Critical analysis, described in Chapter Three, helps us to explore in depth various aspects of our practice. Synoptic analysis helps us to examine, in broad sweeps, the totality of our practice. When we analyze continuing education from a synoptic perspective, we go to disciplines such as psychology, sociology, anthropology, and history that give us multiple perspectives on such topics as adults as learners, the nature of learning, and societal influences on adult learning. We may also go directly to a particular continuing education program and analyze it following a phenomenological approach described later in this chapter. The normative approach, discussed in the last section of this chapter, goes beyond examination and analysis of continuing education to advocating positions, practices, and perspectives. The normative approach attempts to answer the question "What should be?"

Synoptic Approach

Although it is a cliché, the old story about the seven blind men asked to report on their examination of an elephant continues to make an important point. The man who happened to grasp the beast's tail reported quite differently than the man who examined the giant front leg; and the man who felt the elephant's trunk described an elephant far different from the one described by the man who felt the large floppy ear. Yet, without a doubt they were all describing the same beast.

Unfortunately, too often in continuing education we have seen similar fragmented descriptions of a larger whole. The psychologist's view of the adult learner can be quite different from the anthropologist's. And, in a broader sense, those who view continuing education from the perspective of the humanities often view it quite differently than those who view it from the perspective of the social sciences.

Physicist David Bohm (1980) argues that segmentation and specialization of thought and action have been carried too far and have resulted in an often incomplete personal world view.

> This sort of ability of man to separate himself from his environment and to divide and apportion things ultimately led to a wide range of negative and destructive results, because man lost awareness of what he was doing and thus extended the process of division beyond the limits within which it works properly. In essence, the process of division is a way of *thinking about things* that is convenient and useful mainly in the domain of practical, technical, and functional activities (for example, to divide up an area of land into different fields where various crops are to be grown). However, when this mode of thought is applied more broadly to man's notion of himself and the whole world in which he lives (that is, to his self-world view), then man ceases to regard the resulting divisions as merely useful or convenient and begins to see and experience himself and his world as actually constituted of separately existent fragments. Being guided by a fragmentary self-world view, man then acts in such a way as to try to break himself and the world up, so that all seems to correspond to his way of thinking. Man thus obtains an

apparent proof of the correctness of his fragmen-
tary self-world view though, of course, he over-
looks the fact that it is he himself, acting according
to his mode of thought, who has brought about the
fragmentation that now seems to have an autonomous existence, independent of his will and of his
desire [pp. 2-3].

C. P. Snow (1959) pointed up the problem between the
scientists and the humanists, how these two groups have developed a great distrust for each other, and how this rift has often
prevented a broader view of reality. "The nonscientists have a
rooted impression that the scientists are shallowly optimistic,
unaware of man's condition. On the other hand, the scientists
believe that the literary intellectuals [humanists] are totally
lacking in foresight, peculiarly unconcerned with their brother
men, in a deep sense anti-intellectual, anxious to restrict both
art and thought to the existential moment" (p. 5).

Not only has there been a wide split between scientists
and humanists, but there has been reluctance to draw widely
on literature within each of these broad areas of study. For instance, the connections between sociologists and physicists
have been slight; and likewise, the interaction between histor-
ians and philosophers has not been great. These tendencies have
sometimes prevented use of the broad synoptic approach to
viewing situations. If one was trained as a sociologist, for example, it is unlikely that one would draw widely outside of sociology. But that is precisely what I am suggesting is necessary if
one is to analyze continuing education from a synoptic perspective.

Many scholars are beginning to advocate a synoptic view
in intellectual life. For instance, Geertz (1983, p. 19) writes,
"A number of things, I think, are true. One is that there has
been an enormous amount of genre mixing in intellectual life
in recent years, and it is, such blurring of kinds, continuing
apace. Another is that many social scientists have turned away
from a laws and instances ideal of explanation toward a cases
and interpretations one, looking less for the sort of thing that

connects planets and pendulums and more for the sort that connects chrysanthemums and swords. Yet another is that analogies
drawn from the humanities are coming to play the kind of role in
sociological understanding that analogies drawn from the crafts
and technology have long played in physical understanding."

Geertz is saying more than that we must draw widely
from a variety of intellectual pursuits. He is suggesting that
many areas of intellectual inquiry are beginning to mix with one
another and become blurred. Researchers have felt less com-
pelled to stay entirely within the defined limits of their traditional disciplines. "Social scientists have become free to shape
their work in terms of its necessities rather than according to received ideas as to what they ought or ought not be doing. . . .
It has . . . dawned on social scientists that they did not need to
mimic physicists or closet humanists or to invent some new
realm of being to serve as the object of their investigations. Instead they could proceed with their vocation, trying to discover
order in collective life, and decide how what they were doing
was connected to related enterprises" (Geertz, 1983, p. 21).

Peters and Waterman (1982), in their popular book *In
Search of Excellence,* advocate a mixing of intellectual pursuits.
They question analytic approaches that rely heavily on numbers. "The exclusively analytic approach run wild leads to an
abstract, heartless philosophy. Our obsession with body counts
in Viet Nam and our failure to understand the persistence and
long-time horizon of the Eastern mind culminated in America's
most catastrophic misallocation of resources—human, moral,
material" (p. 45). Peters and Waterman also question a totally
rational approach to every situation (suggesting the need to accommodate information that may have intuitive sources). They
argue, "The central problem with the rationalist view of organizing people is that people are not very rational . . . man is the
ultimate study in conflict and paradox" (p. 55).

The physicists have provided us another set of reasons
that we should analyze situations from a synoptic perspective.
Wilbur (1982, p. 3) wrote, "In the explicate or manifest realm
of space and time, things and events are indeed separate and discrete. But beneath the surface, as it were, in the implicate or

frequency realm, all things and events are spacelessly, timelessly, intrinsically, one and undivided." Wilbur is telling us that even though we may wish to divide reality, it is ultimately impossible to do so, for fundamentally everything is connected and related. Wilbur uses the metaphor of the hologram to make his point. "A hologram is a special type of optical storage system that can best be explained by an example: if you take a holographic photo of, say, a horse, and cut out one section of it, for example, the horse's head, and then enlarge that section to the original size, you will get, not a big head, but a picture of the *whole* horse. In other words, each individual part of the picture contains the whole picture in condensed form. The part is in the whole and the whole is in each part—a type of unity-in-diversity and diversity-in-unity. The key point is simply that the *part* has access to the *whole*" (p. 2).

Physicist Fritjof Capra (1975), who writes about the new physics, quantum mechanics, makes a similar point.

> Quantum theory . . . reveals a basic oneness of the universe. It shows that we cannot decompose the world into independently existing smallest units. As we penetrate into matter, nature does not show us any isolated "basic building blocks," but rather appears as a complicated web of relations between the various parts of the whole. These relations always include the observer in an essential way. The human observer constitutes the final link in the chain of observational processes, and the properties of any atomic object can be understood only in terms of the object's interaction with the observer. This means that the classical ideal of an objective description of nature is no longer valid. The Cartesian partition between the I and the world, between the observer and the observed, cannot be made when dealing with atomic matter. In atomic physics, we can never speak about nature without, at the same time, speaking about ourselves [p. 57].

Capra takes our argument one step further. Not only does

he argue that all of nature is related, but he reminds us that when we do an analysis in which we draw on many sources of information, we have brought ourselves into the picture. We cannot remain detached, we cannot be objective. Just as all the pieces we are bringing together are fundamentally related to one another, so are we related to the pieces. Thus any synoptic analysis we do carries our personal stamp—we are a part of the analysis. It is sometimes easy to overlook this most important point.

Educators of adults have long recognized the importance of drawing from other disciplines to gain insight into continuing education. One of the most notable works was a book commissioned by the Professors of Adult Education, *Adult Education: Outlines of an Emerging Field of University Study* (Jensen, Liveright, and Hallenbeck, 1964). Several chapters in this book are devoted to how continuing education "borrows and reformulates knowledge of other disciplines." Discipline areas discussed specifically include sociology, social psychology, psychology, organization and administration, and history.

There are some dangers in wholesale borrowing of concepts from other disciplines. As Robert Boyd and I have pointed out, "There are two arguments against this free borrowing of concepts and theories. First, before we seek help from other disciplines, we must clearly see the unique and particular configurations of adult education as an activity. Second, before borrowing materials, we must establish the similarities and dissimilarities between the context of that material and our own context. We must ask ourselves what erroneous assumptions we may be accepting when we borrow from established disciplines to define problems in adult education. When scholars define the nature of and solutions to problems in their field of study, they are defining that field of study, its premises, mode of argumentation, and criteria for proof. But the methodology of the social and natural sciences is not necessarily appropriate to the problems of adult education" (Boyd, Apps, and Associates, 1980, pp. 2-3). Although these cautions must be considered, we should not avoid examining, and indeed should be encouraged to examine, a broad sweep of literature to gain a fuller understanding of the many aspects and conditions of continuing education.

Some guidelines to follow when examining literature for information and insight about continuing education are these:

1. When examining literature, look broadly, combining information from the arts and the humanities with information from the physical, biological, and social sciences. Particularly look beyond one's own area of specialization.

2. Be not always concerned that information be traceable to a particular disciplinary source. That is, be more concerned with the relation of the information to continuing education than whether it came from sociology, psychology, history, and so on. Oftentimes, as Geertz (1983) pointed out, the source of information will be blurred.

3. Become comfortable with information that has nonrational as well as rational roots. Likewise, become comfortable with information that is quantitative as well as that which does not lend itself to measurement, such as intuitive knowledge.

4. Realize that although much of the knowledge of the world is segmented, the physicists and others are telling us that everything is related and that segmentation is only a practical convenience.

5. Accept the realization that no one can be objective and that when practitioners go in search of information about continuing education, they are directly involved in the process. Ultimately, they are learning about themselves when they attempt to gain a broader perspective about continuing education.

6. Be aware of the problems of borrowing concepts from other disciplines. Compare the context of continuing education with the context of the concept you are interested in borrowing, making certain they are similar.

7. Try to keep a sense of the whole at all times, even though at a given moment you may focus attention on some part of the whole. For example, when examining the aims of continuing education, one must keep in mind the entire continuing education enterprise, adults as learners, content, teaching/learning approaches, and so on.

Phenomenological Approach

This second synoptic approach starts with a particular continuing education situation rather than going to literature for information. Called "phenomenology" (related to the word *phenomenon*), this approach "is the direct investigation and description of phenomena as consciously experienced, without theories about their causal explanation and as free as possible from unexamined preconceptions and presuppositions" (Spiegelberg, 1975, p. 3).

When doing phenomenology, one investigates a phenomenon directly, not relying on words and other symbols that might be used to describe the phenomenon. "To phenomenology the primary stimulus ... is what *is* and what *appears,* not what anyone thinks or says about it" (Spiegelberg, 1975, p. 15). A continuing education phenomenon is examined in as fresh and unencumbered a way as possible. One does not, on experiencing something, immediately begin relating it to some known theory or framework. Further, one attempts to focus on the entirety of the experience, insofar as that is possible, without trying to reduce the experience to a collection of pieces to be examined.

Spiegelberg (1975) discusses six phases when doing phenomenology. He suggests that each phase represents a particular kind of phenomenology, but he also believes the various phases relate to and build on one another. As we examine each phase, we will try to grasp its meaning but also try to show how this particular phase, and eventually the entire process, can assist us in a broad understanding of continuing education. (For our purposes, it makes sense to change the order of Spiegelberg's phases 2 and 3.)

The phases are (1) describing the phenomenon, (2) searching for multiple perspectives, (3) searching for essence and structure, (4) constituting meaning, (5) suspending judgment, and (6) interpreting the phenomenon.

1. *Describing the phenomenon.* A particular experienced event or activity is described as freely as possible. No attempt is made to classify or categorize, but everything described must have an origin in the concrete experience.

Let us take, for example, a two-day conference that focuses on the returning adult student. At the end of the conference we list everything we can think of about the conference. We describe the participants. We note the program plan. We write down reactions we hear from people about the conference. We record our own reactions to various phases of the conference. We gather as much information as we can, without trying to fit it into categories or into any theory of conference planning. We pay particular attention to subjective data we can gather, as well as information about meanings and values. As Spiegelberg points out, we should go beyond talking about values using the word *values*. "Rather than using such threadbare and colorless terms as *value* and pale general predicates as *good* and *bad* we should begin with the concrete experiences of our delights and disgusts, admirations and indignations. The phenomena which give rise to these experiences are the delightful and the disgusting, the admirable and the outrageous. These are the concrete bases for our experiences of value and disvalue. . . . The important thing is that the descriptive approach can salvage and reveal a richness of qualities which the impoverished talk about values as merely a matter of likes or dislikes misses completely" (p. 60).

All of us need to increase our ability to describe our experiences richly and precisely, avoiding "shorthand" words that are bland and have little meaning. By following the descriptive phase of phenomenology, we can develop a new appreciation for those activities that are a part of our lives as educators of adults. But to do justice to this first phase, we must learn to describe beyond the superficial, the "facts" of the situation. We must become comfortable recording our feelings and impressions as well.

2. *Searching for multiple perspectives.* "Phenomenology pays attention not only to the *what* but also the *how,* to the ways or modes in which the phenomena appear. In so doing, it watches particularly the different aspects under which an object with its many sides presents itself, for example, its perspectives shadings, . . . its degree of clearness, its illumination, and so on" (Spiegelberg, 1975, pp. 64-65).

To use a homey example, when we view fish swimming in

a fish tank from the side, we capture one set of images; when we view the same fish tank from the end, the images are different; when we view the tank from the top and from the bottom, we again gather quite different images of the tank, of the water, of the plants that may be present, and, of course, of the fish. A fish viewed head on appears to us quite differently than when viewed from the side—a common way to portray fish.

Likewise, when we reflect on a given continuing education event, situation, or phenomenon, we can gain multiple views if we seek out multiple perspectives. Let us say, for example, that we want to improve a noncredit course we have been teaching. We would obtain information from the participants and from reflecting on our perception of what occurred. We could also seek information from an observer we ask to visit our class, from participants in previous classes, and so on. We try to gain information from as many perspectives as possible, conscious that the information from various sources may conflict. Participants' reactions to the class will likely be different partway through the course, when the course ends, and a month later. Our own perception of this class may be different at the time it ends and a month later.

A key to searching for multiple perspectives is to try to make the usual unusual; that is, search for perspectives to viewing a phenomenon that go beyond what we usually do. The variety of perspectives with which phenomena may be viewed is nearly inexhaustible.

3. *Searching for essence and structure.* During this phase we try to grasp the structures of the event, activity, or other phenomenon we have experienced and the relationships within and among these structures. Here is where intuitive knowledge can come into play. As we reflect on an experience, we attempt to ferret out structures and relationships. But as I said earlier, no insight into structures and relationships can be accepted without backing by specific examples from the experience. "If intuiting essences requires constant reference to concrete examples, then essential thinking is anything but a flight from concreteness. It calls for a constant mobilization of our imagination. Thus, contrary to common belief, essential insight will not

lead us to indulging in empty abstractions but to shuttling back and forth between the concrete and the abstract" (Spiegelberg, 1975, p. 63).

Following our example of the conference on returning adult students, after completing phase 2, we would examine the various types of data we have collected and begin to put pieces together into structures. Let us assume, of course, that the purpose of doing the phenomenology is to improve future conferences. We might discover, on examining our data, that we have categories of data such as conflict in program purposes, participant unease, budget difficulties, and promotion dilemmas. As we reflect on what we have observed and the comments we have obtained, we begin to see these and other categories emerge. We also begin to see relationships among the categories. Some obvious connections are made—budget difficulties related to participant unease, for instance. As we reflect on the data and the results of our phase 1 analysis, we concentrate on allowing the structures and relationships among structures to emerge, always being careful not to develop structures prematurely. We also avoid trying to force data into categories that are selected before reflecting on the data.

4. *Constituting meaning.* During this phase we go beyond our initial attempts to develop structures and relationships to a more in-depth examination of structure, focusing on how the structure of a particular phenomenon formed in our consciousness. During this phase we are conscious of the unique relationship of the knower to the known.

For instance, when we first read a book that we are reviewing, we obtain some early impression of its structure and essence. Later, when we read some parts of the book again and begin reflecting on what the book is saying, we move to a deeper level of consciousness about the structure and essence of the book. We begin to bring into our analysis a relationship of who we are to the essence of the book. Or, when we reflect on a policy statement our agency has recently produced, after working through phases 1 through 3 we begin to examine how we, as unique educators of adults, relate to this policy statement.

5. *Suspending judgment.* We must always suspend our

judgment while we are collecting information and beginning to become acquainted with a continuing education activity. We must stand back from the activity so that we can view it in a fresh way, rather than be encumbered by theories and beliefs that direct perception. "Suspending our belief in the reality of the outside world on the ground of its dubitability is an act of intellectual self-discipline. In a sense it is an attempt to push skepticism to its utmost limits" (Spiegelberg, 1975, p. 68). *Bracketing* is another term used to indicate suspending beliefs about phenomena and allowing the phenomena we are investigating to speak to us directly.

For example, if we wish to examine the adult learner following this approach, we will set aside the various human development theories, the psychological theories of learning, and our own beliefs about adults as learners, and we will let our experience in working with adult learners speak to us directly, following phases 1 through 4 as just discussed. By following this bracketing procedure, we will come to know the adult learner in a fresh, unencumbered way. We will also, according to the phenomenologists, see aspects of the adult learner that we might not have seen had we tried to fit our observations into our previous beliefs and into known theories.

6. *Interpreting the phenomenon.* Also known as hermeneutic phenomenology, this process involves interpreting phenomena in a way that allows hidden meanings to emerge. Descriptive phenomenologists believed that one should abide by what was immediately given. Spiegelberg believes it is possible to go further than merely describing phenomena. "There is at least a possibility of extending the conception of phenomenology in such a way that it can give us access to meanings of the phenomena which are not directly perceived" (1975, p. 69). Thus we are encouraged, once we have worked our way through phases 1 through 5, to reflect on the rich information we have obtained and to try to derive meaning from our reflection that goes deeper than the obvious, surface meanings presented by the information we have accumulated.

For instance, let us assume we are analyzing an institutional policy statement, following the five phases just outlined. We detect, after careful inspection, that the statement is establishing some new direction that will affect what we do. But after reflecting on the information for a time, we begin to perceive some deeper meanings that are not immediately apparent when reading the document. We discover that although the statement does not say so directly, a changed set of priorities will occur in our institution. After careful reflection, it appears that the program areas that have had highest priorities have been replaced by other priorities. We arrive at this decision only after considerable thought about the information we have.

Normative Approach

When we follow the normative approach, we make statements about future direction and action; we try to answer the question of what should be. Some educators of adults have not been shy in making such pronouncements. One has only to go to the literature of adult and continuing education to find pages of normative statements. For instance, Paulo Freire (1970, p. 85) advocates a particular approach to adult education. He writes: "The starting point for organizing the program content of education or political action must be the present, existential, concrete situation, reflecting the aspirations of the people. Utilizing certain basic contradictions, we must pose this existential, concrete, present situation to the people as a problem which challenges them and requires a response—not just at the intellectual level, but at the level of action."

Ivan Illich (1971, p. 75) makes clear what he believes should be the purpose of an educational system: "It should provide all who want to learn with access to available resources at any time in their lives; empower all who want to share what they know to find those who want to learn it from them; and, finally, furnish all who want to present an issue to the public with the opportunity to make their challenge known."

Paul Bergevin (1967, p. 4) advocates a particular stance toward the process of learning: "We must learn that how we are taught is as important as what we are taught. We must learn to feel responsible for the success of the learning adventure by becoming involved in the dynamics of the adult learning process."

Some educators of adults have written about future direction, perhaps none more eloquently than Eduard Lindeman ([1926] 1961, p. 4): "The spirit and meaning of education cannot be enhanced by addition, by the easy method of giving the same dose to more individuals. If learning is to be revivified, quickened so as to become once more an adventure, we shall have need of new concepts, new motives, new methods; we shall need to experiment with the qualitative aspects of education."

Others have listed principles that ought to be followed. Leon McKenzie (1978, pp. 62–67) says: "(1) Education should facilitate in adults a rejection of historical determinism in any form . . . (2) Education should facilitate in adults the development of personal autonomy . . . (3) Education should facilitate in adults the courage to become . . . (4) Education must facilitate in adults a concern for human welfare, a planetary consciousness . . . (5) Education must facilitate in adults a spirit of interdependence and collaborativeness."

These are but a few examples of normative, or "should be," statements. In later chapters positions advocated by many others both in and outside the field of continuing education will be presented.

The normative view has often been expressed by educational philosophers through the development of philosophies of education. For example, in *Toward a Working Philosophy of Adult Education* (1973) I discussed the classic educational philosophies of essentialism, perennialism, progressivism, reconstructionism, and existentialism. Each of these philosophies has a particular view on the nature of human beings as learners, on the teaching/learning process, on aims of educational activities, on the role of content in education, and on the role for the educator.

More recently, Elias and Merriam (1980) have developed a list of philosophies of adult education. These include the liberal, the progressive, the behaviorist, the humanistic, the radical, and the analytic philosophies of adult education. The problem with all these philosophies (with the exception of Elias and Merriam's analytic philosophy, which is process-oriented) is that they can prevent analysis and original thought. Once one reads through a description of these various philosophies, the tendency is to try to fit one's own philosophy into one of these established philosophies. Once one has done so, the inclination is to become comfortable with this new-found intellectual home and stop questioning and challenging and constantly searching for new positions. The normative statement made by this book is that we as practitioners in continuing education must always remain critical of our practice, asking questions and seeking answers. We cannot retreat into someone else's philosophy as a kind of storm cellar that protects us from facing our practice head on.

When making normative statements, guidelines to consider include the following:

1. Do not hesitate to make statements that suggest what ought to be—a future statement about the direction of your agency, for example, or statements about how you believe programs should be planned, how adults should be taught, about the aims for continuing education programs.

2. Normative statements must be guided by a careful analysis of the situation, an informed view of like situations, and a knowledge of the related literature. Normative statements should not be made without a foundation. (Unfortunately, many times they are.) The processes for analysis discussed in Chapter Three and the approach to examining literature and situations (synoptic approach) discussed earlier in this chapter can serve as foundations for making normative statements.

3. Avoid being trapped into accepting someone else's philosophy as your own. It is easy to say that you subscribe to a humanistic philosophy of adult education or that you belong to the progressivist philosophy. More important, one's normative statements should reflect one's own analysis and study. Someone else's philosophy can provide an interesting comparison and can illustrate how someone else has worked out viewpoints on various aspects of continuing education. Ultimately, though, each of us must do his or her own analysis and reach his or her own conclusions.

Summary

The synoptic approach to examining continuing education encourages us to look at the field broadly, drawing on such disciplines as psychology, sociology, anthropology, and history. Several quantum mechanics physicists argue that it is impossible to consider anything in isolation without realizing that it is a part of a whole. Hence it is reasonable to believe that when examining any segment of continuing education, one must be aware of a total context. A synoptic approach to continuing education can also include examining an event or activity following some of the procedures suggested by phenomenology.

The normative approach means making "should be" statements about continuing education practice. As practitioners, we should not avoid doing this. But normative statements must be informed by a careful attention to analytic and synoptic procedures.

Existing philosophies of education such as essentialism and progressivism can give us information about how others have viewed assumptions about learning, learners, aims, and so forth. But we must avoid accepting one of these philosophies as our own without accepting the responsibility for examining our own practice—and ourselves—and then making our own normative statements.

5

Discovering New Ways to View Adult Learners

~~~~~~

In the previous four chapters, we examined a process for analyzing continuing education practice following critical, synoptic, and normative analysis approaches. In this and succeeding chapters I will show how to apply these approaches when examining continuing education practice.

This chapter focuses on adults as learners. Chapter Six examines aims for continuing education. Chapter Seven illustrates how to analyze teaching and learning. Chapter Eight looks at content and program planning, and Chapter Nine demonstrates how to analyze continuing education policy. Each of these chapters represents an example of how one might analyze that particular aspect of practice. The chapters are not intended to include all the issues and problems worthy of analysis. Rather, the intent is, by way of example, to show how one might carry out an analysis of one's practice. The analyses illustrated are certainly not the only ones. Each of us, as we do an analysis of our practice, will select different features to analyze.

To begin, let us look in on Greg Ashley and some of the problems and challenges he faces at Westwind College. (Both Ashley and Westwind are fictitious, representing a composite of continuing education programs and practitioners.)

Case Study

Greg Ashley has been director of continuing education at Westwind College for three years. Westwind is a small liberal arts college in the Midwest, located in a city with a population of 65,000. The college has been involved in continuing education programs from the time it began, yet little thought has ever been given to the direction for continuing education programming. It mostly just happened. A faculty member wanted to offer a course off campus, and it was offered. Several faculty members came up with an idea for a conference, and because they could show no cost to the institution, the conference was held. An assistant to the president did the little coordinating of continuing education activities that took place. During the last few years, though, with a somewhat depressed enrollment of traditional-age students, the administration and the board decided to remodel the continuing education program and give it direction. The hope was to increase enrollments in both credit and noncredit courses. At least these were the dreams Westwind's administrators and board members shared with Ashley when he started at Westwind. Before arriving at Westwind, Ashley had five years' experience as an assistant director of continuing education at an eastern university.

When he arrived at Westwind, Ashley found a faculty that was somewhat suspicious of the continuing education program and the students it attracted. When Ashley began visiting offices, meeting the faculty members and trying to find out which ones might be interested in teaching in the continuing education program, he met Amos Smith, an English professor with thirty years' experience, most of it at Westwind.

"Ashley," Smith said, after they had talked for a bit, "Those adult education students are of three types—all bad for the image of this college. First, there are the women whose husbands make good money, and they don't know what to do with their time. So they enroll in these continuing education courses we sponsor—gives them something to do. Then there's a group of older students who goofed off when they were in college the first time, and now they want to take some courses at night and on weekends to make up for their past mistakes. The third group is working people, both men and women, who see this college as a place where they can pick up some personal skill courses—how to write better, how to speak better, how to do their jobs better. These are people who think that we're some kind of vocational school and that we can help them make more money. Most of them haven't read a book in years, outside of some shoot-'em-up western or a romance novel—and they probably won't, either. They aren't interested in an education, they just want to make more money on the job."

Ashley listened carefully to the English professor's litany but did not argue. He wondered at the time how many other professors felt as Amos Smith did. As he became acquainted with the faculty, he soon discovered that many professors shared Smith's feelings about the continuing education students and the classes, courses, workshops, and other programs in which they enrolled. Ashley had expected to meet some negative reaction, but he was surprised at how strong it was. Nevertheless, with the support of the administration and the board he began promoting his programs and soon saw some modest increases in enrollments.

Then he met Susan Hanson, who had recently been hired as a sociology instructor. Over coffee one day, Ashley and Hanson were discussing the kinds of students in Westwind's continuing education program. "Sounds like typical continuing education students to me," Hanson offered. "Except where are those interested in world affairs, in national issues, in local issues and concerns? Aren't there some of those people living in this community? I haven't heard you mention them."

Ashley reflected on her analysis for a moment and decided she was right. He could not identify any in Westwind's various continuing education offerings that focused on issues, and thus it was understandable that Hanson knew of no continuing education students with such interests.

Not dissuaded by what he had heard from fellow faculty members at Westwind, Ashley developed a formal needs analysis survey to find out the characteristics of the people who lived in the community and to determine their needs and problems.

Ashley was committed to developing a continuing education program based on needs of the people. He mailed 3,000 questionnaires to a random sample of people in the community and received 800 replies. He discovered that the family income level of those replying ranged from low to quite high, with a median family income comparable to the figures for his state. Average educational level was 13.5 years. About 15 percent of those replying were minorities. About 25 percent answering the survey said they were now attending some type of continuing education program.

With his survey findings in mind, Ashley launched a vigorous promotion campaign for Westwind's continuing education program. He bought ads in the local newspaper; he developed spot announcements for radio and television. He prepared brochures and placed them in libraries and in dentists' and doctors' offices in the community. He arranged to be invited to meetings of service clubs that met in the community. He wrote news stories describing the various continuing education programs Westwind had developed.

A few days after his third anniversary at Westwind, Ashley met with President Harrison Williams to discuss the continuing education program and its future. Ashley was somewhat disappointed with the results of his extensive marketing effort. In fact, Williams reminded him that the promotional costs likely exceeded the revenue obtained from the new participants. Ashley also reflected on faculty attitudes toward continuing education and decided they had changed little if at all. Many faculty members either completely ignored continuing education activities and participants or were hostile toward the program.

Ashley also shared with Williams a survey he had just completed of persons participating in Westwind's continuing education program. The survey showed the following: women, 60 percent; men, 40 percent; age groups represented—eighteen to twenty-four, 35 percent; thirty-five to forty-four, 30 percent; forty-five to fifty-four, 27 percent; fifty-five and over, 8 percent; minority group participation, 5 percent. Twenty-one percent of the participants were college graduates. Only 10 percent had less than a high school diploma.

At the meeting with Williams, the two of them decided President Williams would appoint a task force of program participants, faculty members, and community leaders to draft a statement for Westwind's future continuing education activities. Within three months the task force completed its task and presented its position paper. One section of the task force paper was titled "Target Participants" and read:

> The target groups for Westwind's continuing education program include all the citizens living in reasonable traveling distance of Westwind's campus, plus those to whom programs can be delivered with Westwind's various media outlets and its correspondence program.
>
> A special attempt must be made to reach those educational consumers who do not participate in large numbers, such as those with limited formal education and those with low incomes. A new marketing strategy must be developed to bring the nonparticipants into the program. We have a reputation at Westwind for high-quality programs in the arts and the humanities. With very little investment risk, but with faculty commitment, we can offer many of our programs in the arts and humanities to new adult publics in our community. Through an active, well-conceived continuing education program, Westwind's regular academic faculty resources can be extended to these new publics. Westwind's motto for its continuing education program is "Of Service to All—We Meet Needs."

We might summarize Westwind's continuing education program in this way:

1. Enrollments of adults in Westwind's various offerings are not as great as expected.
2. Some campus faculty members hold negative feelings about continuing education programs and their participants.
3. Westwind's continuing education program, though appar-

ently based on a needs analysis, is not as well received in
the community as expected.

4. Westwind faculty members teaching in continuing educa-
    tion appear not interested in social concerns and issues.
5. Something was probably wrong with the promotion cam-
    paign that Ashley followed in trying to recruit new stu-
    dents.
6. Minority representation in Westwind's continuing educa-
    tion program is much lower than the proportion of minori-
    ties in the community.
7. Persons with less than twelve years of formal schooling are
    not participating to the same extent as those with twelve
    years and over of formal schooling.
8. Men and persons fifty-five and over are underrepresented in
    Westwind's continuing education programs.

Critical Analysis

Let us begin our analysis of adults as learners, as evident
in the Westwind case study, by listing several assumptions.
Many assumptions could be listed, but I will mention only those
that seem most important. From what Ashley and Williams have
said and done, it would appear these men assumed the following about adult learners:

1. Adult learners are participants. To learn, an adult enrolls in
    some type of class, course, workshop—an activity in which
    the adult is a participant.
2. They are consumers of knowledge provided by educational
    institutions such as Westwind.
3. They will enroll in an educational program if they learn
    about its existence. The better an adult/continuing educa-
    tion program is promoted, the more people will attend. A
    related assumption is that adults of various formal educa-
    tional levels and income levels will be attracted to the same
    educational offerings.
4. They are primarily rational, know what problems they face,
    and are able to identify their educational "needs" through
    a formal needs analysis.

From comments Amos Smith, the English professor, offered, we can deduce he likely assumes that adult learners (1) are academically marginal and (2) either are enrolling in educational activities as a leisure-time activity, are pursuing education to correct earlier inadequate schooling, or are interested in education from a purely vocational perspective.

The comments of Susan Hanson, the sociology instructor, suggest she assumes some continuing education faculty members and students should be interested in local, state, and national issues and in policy questions and activities related to these issues.

Let us examine these assumptions—first, the assumption that adult learners are participants. This is a common, often unstated assumption for anyone who works for an agency or institution that sponsors educational programs for adults. One important way for an adult to learn something, many believe, is to participate in a program. Yet, when we examine the literature of adult/continuing education, we discover that only about one third of all adults participate in organized learning and organized instruction (Cross, 1981, p. 52). A much larger group, 70 percent, organize and carry out their own self-directed learning (Tough, 1971, p. 1). Most of those who participate in organized programs also conduct their own self-directed learning.

These findings suggest that many people learn outside organized educational settings. They are usually able to plan their own learning in a way that is far less expensive than if they had gone to an educational provider, and besides, their self-directed learning project has likely provided them exactly what they wanted to learn.

But the research shows us something else about who participates. The several research projects that have examined participation patterns have all found that amount of formal schooling is the one factor that has more influence than any other (Johnstone and Rivera, 1965; Anderson and Darkenwald, 1979). The more formal schooling a person has, the more likely the learner will participate in organized adult/continuing education activities. To go further, we could hypothesize that those with greater amounts of schooling are more comfortable with schooling than those with lesser amounts. They stayed in the class-room longer and thus like what happens in a classroom.

Let us examine Ashley's and Williams's assumptions 2 and 3 together—adults as consumers of knowledge and the dependence of number of participants on how well we promote (market) programs. As we reflect on these two assumptions, we can relate them to the factory metaphor often used in adult/continuing education. Knowledge is viewed as a product that is "marketed" through various promotional approaches to consumers (adult learners). Several assumptions are embedded within the factory metaphor. First is that it is possible to "package" knowledge in such a way that it can be "delivered" to consumers (adult learners) who will "buy" the knowledge (pay fees or tuition). Second, for the factory (adult education agency or institution) to stay in operation, it must continue to attract consumers to its product. Third, increasingly attractive means must be employed to encourage consumers to want to purchase the product of a given agency or institution because there are many competitors in the marketplace.

We could go on with examples of the factory metaphor, but let us stop and reflect on what they mean. What inherent view of human nature do we hold when we accept the view that adult learners are consumers of knowledge and that our task as educators is to encourage them to participate (to purchase our commodity)? And what view do we hold about the nature of teaching and learning and about knowledge when we accept the adult learner as consumer of knowledge? (More about this in succeeding chapters.)

As I argued earlier, what if the person is not inclined to participate in a course, class, or workshop? What if the person prefers to learn by himself or herself? Are we prepared to accommodate this person? What if the person cannot afford our fees? What if the person is forced, through some mandatory educational requirements posed by a profession or employer, to participate in certain types of educational activities? The question then becomes, is it always (or ever) appropriate to view the adult learner as consumer?

Further, is it appropriate to call promotion of institutionally sponsored education "marketing?" Does the word *market-ing*, because it has roots in the factory metaphor, engender a meaning different from what we intend?

Kotler (1975) believes that nonprofit organizations, including educational institutions, can benefit greatly from marketing. He writes: "Exchange is the central concept underlying marketing. It calls for the offering of value to someone in exchange for value. . . . A professional marketer is someone who is very good at *understanding, planning, and managing exchanges.* He knows how to research and understand the needs of the other party; to design a valued offering to meet these needs; to communicate the offer effectively; and to present it in a good place and under timely circumstances" (p. 5).

It seems plausible that certain practices from marketing are applicable in adult/continuing education. But by calling these practices "marketing," are we leaving the impression that we are no different from a factory that produces a product, markets it to consumers, and gains a reasonable profit from the activity? Is this the image we wish to communicate?

Do we accept the assumption that Williams and Ashley held about adults being rational and knowing the problems they face? This question has been debated at length in recent years. Do adults really know their problems and needs well enough so they can express them? Those who believe in needs-analysis strategies obviously believe they can. But many others, such as Freire (1973), believe that many people are socialized to be unable to express the problems and needs that are most fundamental in their lives. Freire points out that for a variety of reasons many persons, particularly many low-income and minority persons, are not able to communicate their needs or problems. In some instances they may even fear communicating the needs and problems that are most fundamental in their lives. Freire advocates a consciousness-raising process designed to help individuals become aware of the more fundamental problems in their lives. This process involves small groups of persons discussing problems and needs.

Moreover, is it safe to assume that adults usually enroll in a continuing education activity because it reflects some need they want satisfied? To what extent do people enroll for non-educational-need-related reasons: "That course sounds interesting, I'll enroll"; "My friend is enrolling, I'll go with her"; "The workshop meets when I have some free time"? As Bock (1980) points out, "A range of personal and situational reasons influence the decision to participate. Some of the important reasons for participating in an educational activity are related to the benefits an individual receives for participating, such as interest in the subject matter or enjoyment of the method of learning, the setting, or the interaction with other people" (pp. 129–130).

When we begin to analyze Amos Smith's assumptions, our analysis takes us in another direction. Smith helps us focus on several points about adults as learners and about the role of colleges and universities in adult/continuing education. The literature of adult education points out clearly that adult learners are serious and that they pursue education for a variety of "legitimate" reasons (Apps, 1981; Cross, 1981). Even though research largely refutes the assumptions Smith and many others hold about adult learners, there remain many instructors, particularly in higher education, who believe as Smith does. As continuing education practitioners, we can ask these questions about Professor Smith: (1) Why does he believe what he does about adult learners? (2) What purpose does he see for colleges and universities? Does this include in any way the education of adults? (3) What does Smith believe about an adult's potential for serious learning? From his comments it would appear he believes adults are not capable of much more than recreational or job-related learning.

Susan Hanson's comments cause us to think in yet another direction. Hanson assumes that at least a certain proportion of adult learners are interested in policy questions and issues at various levels. Yet she has pointed out to Ashley that none of Westwind's students are identifiable as having these interests. We could ask several questions: (1) Is it an appropriate role for colleges and universities to offer programs designed particularly for community activists? (2) Are there more than a handful of adult learners who really care about policy decisions and policy making? (3) Should a college or university or any other adult education provider encourage adults' participation in policy questions?

As we reflect on the entire case study, what view of the adult as learner emerges? We have already identified such positions as the adult as consumer, the adult as recipient, and the adult learner as participant. But let us look in greater depth.

To understand the nature of the adult learner at a more fundamental level, we can ask about the nature of human nature and consider the answers the question evokes. Researchers and writers who have explored human behavior can give us insights. Sigmund Freud, for instance, believed that human beings were the product of evolution. (He was, of course, not alone in that belief, as he and others were influenced by Charles Darwin's work.) Freud argued: "Man is not a being different from animals or superior to them; he himself originates in the animal race and is related more closely to some of its members and more distantly to others" ([1925] 1958, p. 6). Freud believed that adult human behavior was largely the result of what had occurred in early childhood. He also held a quite negative view of humankind: "Men are not gentle creatures who want to be loved, and who at the most can defend themselves if they are attacked; they are, on the contrary, creatures among whose instinctual endowments is to be reckoned a powerful share of aggressiveness" ([1930] 1961, p. 58).

Many people in the world today agree with Freud's view about the aggressive nature of humankind. One has only to note the huge defense budgets of many countries of the world to see evidence of this belief. As educators, how do we view the basic human nature of adult learners? And what is our perception of the adult learner's view of us? One dimension of these questions is trust. Do we trust our students? Do they trust us? Trust is considered here as a basic value, a sense of openness between people, a willingness to share, a willingness to be authentic, a concern for fairness, a belief in the fundamental value of each human being.

Many educators would say immediately, "Of course I trust my students and they trust me." But is practice consistent with this statement? Reflect on the case study at the beginning of the chapter. Does Professor Smith trust adult students? I would say not.

A second view of human nature is that held by the behaviorists. The behaviorist view of human nature, a perspective that has grown in prominence during the past fifty years, has been foundational to many adult/continuing education programs. One has only to examine programmed learning, the roots of behavioral objectives, the foundation of behavior modification, or the assumptions behind measuring adult performance levels to see evidence of the behaviorist view of human nature in practice.

B. F. Skinner (1953), a contemporary advocate of behaviorism with many followers, believes human beings do not have freedom to act but behave because of external influences. This view of human nature can be summarized as follows: "The assumption as to human nature is that it is malleable clay awaiting the hand of the behavioral artisan, and the ambition as to the future is to design a technology that will . . . not enhance the freedom and dignity of individuals . . . but 'shape the behavior of members of a group so they will function smoothly for the benefit of all' " (Matson, 1976, pp. 125–126).

For some people, the behaviorist view leads to a view of human behavior as machinelike. This view has gained prominence in the early 1980s as computers have moved into homes and offices. As people have gained an understanding of computers and the logic of their operation, it has been easy to view humans as one kind of computer. We often hear the brain referred to as a computer. Often we go the next step, particularly so far as education is concerned, and say that with this kind of input we can expect that kind of output. Or, with this type of teaching, we can expect that type of behavior to result.

A third view of humankind, one that in large measure has developed as a response to both Freudian and behavioral views, is often called the humanistic view of human beings. The so-called humanistic psychologists such as Gordon Allport (1955), Victor Frankl (1963), Carl Rogers (1961), Erich Fromm (1968), and Abraham Maslow (1968, 1970) subscribe to a view of human nature that underlines trust, freedom for individuals, striving for self-actualization (Maslow), searching for meaning (Frankl), and the unique nature of each human being. Matson (1976, p. xxi) sums up a humanistic view this way: "What is distinctive about man is the power to choose, the freedom to say yes or no to the universe. . . . What is characteristic of the animal is its will to survive, to maintain its existence; but what is characteristic of man is the need to go beyond survival, to risk his own existence, to 'follow all of his days something that he cannot name'—to climb the next mountain, to fly to the moon, to dare the universe, to defy the gods. This is what it means to be a creator: to act upon the world rather than to be acted on, to take chances and to make changes."

It is difficult to discuss "one" humanistic view of human nature, although the several views have commonalities. In addition to the psychologists, persons such as Paulo Freire (1970, 1973) subscribe to a humanistic view of human nature. Freire assumes the following about human nature: "Human beings are free to act on their world. They have the alternative of being able to create and modify their world and themselves, as compared to animals who lack this ability. People are able to reflect on their past, be conscious of the present, and make plans for the future. Nevertheless, we are historical and social beings. Our actions and reflections occur within specific social situations and, to an extent, are limited by these situations" (Apps, 1979, p. 123).

Given these three broad views of human nature, let us once more reflect on the Westwind case study to see how understanding these views might help us comprehend how the people at Westwind view adults as learners. To which of these views do Ashley, Williams, and the persons who wrote the policy statement subscribe? With the limited information we have available, we cannot be sure. But it appears, from the way they talk about adult learners, that they subscribe to a behaviorist view of human nature. What evidence is there for saying this? Let us examine the task force paper again. The drafters of this paper emphasized the need to "reach" those who "do not participate," particularly "those with limited formal education and those with low incomes." The implication is that these people are deficient in education and that with more of it they can increase their incomes and become more productive citizens. The situation can be compared to a machine that is not up to full production and must be repaired or at least fine-tuned in order to produce more. The adult learner, like the machine, is deficient, and participation in educational activities such as those sponsored by Westwind will help correct the situation.

We could also argue that Ashley and Williams hold a humanistic view of human nature, in addition to seeing human beings as machines. Ashley has organized a variety of educational offerings, and he has called to the attention of people in the community what his program has to offer. People are not required to attend anything offered by Westwind; they have the freedom to pick and choose what they wish. They obviously have the opportunity to enroll in courses other than those offered by Westwind and to organize their own learning projects aside from what Westwind and other educational agencies and institutions make available.

From this discussion we see the possibility for individuals to hold more than one view of human nature simultaneously. We should also point out the dangers in attempting to label a person's beliefs about human nature from limited information. One further caution—what one says and what one does are not always the same. For instance, the words a person uses in policy statements and in describing what he or she does may not be consistent with the practice the person follows. To do a thorough job of analyzing how a person views adults as learners, that person's words as well as actions must be observed over an extended period. Nevertheless, it is possible to gain hints and often some strong sense of what a person believes about adults by analyzing what the person says about adults as learners. This is particularly so if we concentrate our attention on the subtleties of the language—the metaphors and slogans used, for instance. Persons may say that they believe adults are free and are self-directing, but they use expressions like "These people need retooling" or "If we are to have competent professionals in our community, they must be required to keep up to date."

Besides asking questions about the nature of human beings, we must also ask about values, ethics, and esthetics. We could ask several ethical questions:

1. Is it ethical to market educational programs to people who may gain little value from them? That is, is it ethical to try to convince people they "need" an educational program when they may not have thought so until they came in contact with the promotional material? Is this approach to promotion any different from that used by hard-sell salespeople who try to convince a person to buy something when that person has never thought before of buying it?

Vance Packard (1957) called the marketers "probers" and wrote, "Certain of the probers, for example, are systematically feeling out our hidden weaknesses and frailties in the hope that they can more efficiently influence our behavior" (p. 5).

Kotler (1975) also calls attention to ethical questions of marketing educational programs. He mentions two areas of ethical concern: (1) the intrusiveness of marketing activity into people's personal affairs and (2) the often manipulative nature of marketing. Of the first point, Kotler writes, "The marketing researcher goes into homes and asks people about their likes and dislikes, their perceptions, their incomes, and other personal matters" (1975, p. 12). Related to the second point, Kotler cautions, "Administrators should be sensitive to the possible charge of manipulation when they implement a marketing program" (p. 12).

Should the word *marketing* be used when talking about educational programs? Is not the word so loaded with hidden meanings and perceptions that we had best use other language when describing our educational programs to adult learners? Kotler, of course, thinks otherwise, as do many administrators of educational programs for adults. What impressions do we leave with persons who might consider enrolling in our various offerings when we talk about marketing? We come back to our original question: What are the ethics of marketing adult/continuing education programs, including using the word *marketing*, and adopting its business strategies?

2. Is it ethical not to inform people of something that might clearly benefit them when they might not be aware of the potential benefits? For instance, let us say one of Ashley's programmers offers a course on microcomputer word processing for business middle managers. Few of the middle managers are aware that microcomputer word processing is something they should consider. Yet, the course promotion material points out the values of microcomputer word processing, and several middle managers enroll. Was it ethical to promote this course by pointing out benefits that middle managers might gain by enrolling? Was it ethical for the Westwind programmer to, in a sense, create a market for this course?

3. Assuming that we would accept both questions 1 and 2 as ethical concerns, is it reasonable to search out some middle ground that would allow us to answer both questions yes? That is, can our promotional activities be ethical from the perspective of not creating needs as well as being reasonable for calling people's attention to program areas of which they are not aware? The quandary is finding the middle ground, particularly in an era when participant numbers are so important to the survival of many continuing education programs. The tendency is to err in the direction of creating markets and perhaps enrolling people in courses, classes, and workshops that offer few benefits to them.

As we examine the Westwind policy statement, we could ask, is it ethical to promote adult education programs with the clear intent that enrollments are necessary to meet budget demands? One sentence in the policy statement, for example, said, "To ensure head count in Westwind's programs so budget can be met, a new marketing strategy must be developed . . . ." A related question—is it ethical to give primary attention to institutional survival over concern for adult learners? The policy statement clearly emphasizes institution over learners. But we must also ask, is it ethical to ignore institutional survival in order to give primary attention to learners? It seems clear that if the institution fails to survive, learners will suffer from lack of opportunity.

Ethical questioning and ethical decision making are seldom easy. They often involve a variety of viewpoints, some of them totally opposed to each other.

The critical analysis procedures followed so far in analyzing the Westwind case study have been (1) identifying and analyzing assumptions and (2) raising basic questions. It should be apparent by now that these procedures can be applied to a variety of continuing education settings, not merely to a college like Westwind. The situations will, of course, be different, but the principles for doing a critical analysis of our practice remain constant, as do many of the issues about the adult as learner.

Up to this point, we have focused our attention on critical analysis of the Westwind situation, with particular attention to the adult as learner. We have looked at the situation from the perspective of identifying assumptions and asking metaphysical and ethical questions. There are a number of additional critical analysis approaches we could have used. We could have examined the definitions used, either implicitly or explicitly, and commented on their adequacy, and we could have examined metaphors and slogans.

After we had done all this, we would know a great deal about Westwind, its programs, its faculty, and its students. We would know a great deal about how this particular institution views the adult as learner, which is the focus of our attention. But we have yet developed no answers to the questions Ashley faces—how to increase enrollments in Westwind's various programs for adults, particularly how to increase participation of those who are less likely to participate, those with low incomes, and those with little formal education. So far, the analysis has opened up a number of areas and likely has created more problems for Ashley than it has solved. That is indeed often the result of doing a critical analysis—new questions emerge, old questions are challenged, and there is a good deal of unease and insecurity about what to do next.

Synoptic Analysis

Following the model presented in Chapter Two, the next phase of our process is synoptic analysis. Synoptic analysis

means obtaining a general view about a particular topic, no matter what its source. In this instance, as we try to find out more
about adults as learners, we can go to a variety of sources. What
follows is not intended to be all-inclusive but merely illustrative
of how one might begin to do a synoptic analysis.

Let us begin by examining a sampling of the psychologists' contributions to the field of adult education. Psychologists have greatly influenced our understanding of adults as
learners, perhaps overly so. Because of their enormous influence, we have often overlooked the contributions of other fields
such as anthropology, sociology, history, physiology, and political science to our understanding of adults as learners.

The life-span researchers (predominantly psychologists)
have provided several models that attempt to explain how
adults change through time. For instance, Buhler (1933/1968)
divided human life into five periods: childhood, self-determina-
tion, stabilization, decline, and retirement. Erikson divided life
into eight stages of ego development (1963, pp. 247–274).
These stages consisted in developing trust, autonomy, initiative,
industry, identity, intimacy, generativity, and integrity. Each of
these eight stages represented a natural progression of change,
and within each stage was a conflict within the self that had to
be resolved. For instance, during early adulthood a person
wrestles with the conflict between intimacy and isolation, and
during middle adulthood the conflict is between generativity
and stagnation.

Havighurst (1963, 1972) divided the life span into six
age periods. For the adult years he identified three periods:
early adulthood (age eighteen to thirty-five), middle age (thirty-
five to sixty), and later maturity (sixty and over). For each
period he listed several tasks to be completed. For instance, a
task of early adulthood was to select a mate, a task of middle
age was to adjust to aging parents, and a task of later maturity
was to adjust to the death of a spouse.

Levinson (1978) examined the lives of forty men between the ages of thirty-five and forty-five and from this examination developed stages of work: selecting and testing an occupation, settling down in the occupation, and reevaluating one's
dream in light of one's attainment.

Each of these models assumes that there is something universal about adults as they age and that these universals can be tied to particular ages. These universals are generally viewed in three categories—physical change, emotional change, and cognitive change.

Many adult educators find these models useful, and some even build their programs around these models, offering particular courses and workshops focusing on particular life-span stages. Yet, many researchers and practitioners alike remain skeptical of some life-span research, such as Levinson's, which focuses on ages and stages and asserts this is the way adults move through life. To explain adulthood as a series of stages through which everyone moves seems overly simplistic and narrow. Can it be expected that every adult will move through life in lockstep, reaching a particular age and then demonstrating a particular set of concerns?

For instance, does every adult face a midlife crisis? Merriam (1979, p. 12) says, "Many writers suggest that crisis is a potentiality rather than a necessity during middle age." Is it also reasonable to assume that everyone moves forward in a linear fashion? Or is it more likely that the movement is in some sort of jagged spiral? Can one's life be seen as a series of movements in a variety of directions, some forward, many backward, with twists and turns that are always evident but never predictable? Brim (1976, p. 8) says, "There is as yet no evidence either for developmental periods or 'stages' in the midlife period, in which one event must come after another, or one personality change brings another in its wake."

Life-span research has given adult educators much. It has shown that adults do not reach some sort of magical maturity that freezes when they reach adulthood, that they indeed change throughout the life span. Thus lifelong learning is an integral part of the human experience—as people change, they learn, and as they learn, they change.

Life-span theories are but one of the many contributions of psychology to understanding adults as learners. Psychology has also given us learning theories, information about adult intelligence and how it changes over the life span, and the effect of various barriers to learning, such as self-concept and fear.

Dušan Savićević (1983), a Yugoslavian researcher, has summarized recent Soviet research about the intellectual development of the adult. With a sample of 2,300 subjects aged eighteen to forty, the Soviet researchers, under the direction of a Soviet psychologist, Ananev, found a rhythmicity to intellectual development. Aspects of intellectual development researched were memory, thinking, and attentiveness. These researchers found that during the period from age eighteen to age twenty-five there are shifting rises and declines of memory, attentiveness, and thinking ability. For instance, attentiveness is rather stable from age eighteen to twenty-one, but from age twenty-two to twenty-five it shows rhythmicity. During the years twenty-six to forty the Soviet researchers reported the maximal development of attentiveness. (The research did not include subjects beyond age forty.) The Soviet researchers also found a strong correlation between the influences of education and learning on the intellectual development of adults—the more learning and education, the greater maintenance of intellectual vigor and stimulation for additional learning.

"The significance of the Soviet investigations is that they give a new image of the potentialities for intellectual development in adults aged eighteen to forty. They have shown that the exercise of intellectual functions, which is attained through learning and education, is the main builder of strength, of skill development, and, gerontologists say, even of longevity. . . . The results obtained present a basis for the restructuring of the existing theory of intellectual development in the adult. Not only do the results point to the possibility of learning during the adult years, but from them it follows that learning and education are absolutely essential to the maintenance of [human beings] and the development of their skills. That, from the standpoint of the realization of the concept of adult education, has a special significance" (Savićević, 1983, p. 197).

But we must not look only to psychology for an understanding of the adult learner. To truly follow what synoptic philosophy teaches, we must look broadly for an understanding of the adult as learner. For example, Knox (1977) summarized adult development research from such perspectives as family role performance; education, work, and community performance; physical condition; personality during adulthood; adult learning; women's roles; and adjusting to change events. Merriam (1979) reviewed a broad range of research on middle age in the categories of career or work factors, family factors, physical aspects, and psychological factors. Both Knox's and Merriam's reviews cut across several disciplines—psychology, sociology, and biology, for instance.

We can look specifically at sociological factors that influence the adult learner. For example, research has shown a strong relationship of income level and of level of formal education and participation in adult education (Cross, 1981, pp. 52-57). Another sociological factor that influences the adult learner is when a person was born. Age cohorts, groups of persons who were born at a particular time, share a common history and cultural development. Adults born and raised during the Depression years of the 1930s bring with them the feelings, values, and concerns they experienced as children; adults who served in World War II, Korea, or Vietnam have the influences of a war as a part of them; adults who attended college during the 1960s were influenced by the protest movement; and so on.

A study of the biology of human aging tells us about changes in reaction time and changes in ability to see and hear (Apps, 1981, pp. 85-87).

History influences our understanding of adult learners. A review of history reveals which areas of study were believed appropriate for women and which were not—nursing, teaching, and clerical areas were commonly accepted. Today, of course, women share with men in the study of most topics. But the historical remnants persist, and women continue to fight prejudice in work and learning situations alike. Many other historical examples could be mentioned. At one time, gaining a college degree was viewed as the end of formal education—the person knew what he or she needed to know. Some adults today still carry the belief that a formal education is sufficient and that further education is not necessary. The historical relationship of economic class to education influenced who received formal education—those from higher income levels went to college, others went immediately into the work force. With the strong relationship between formal education and participation in adult education, this historical fact helps us to understand why many adults who come from low-income families and do not have college degrees do not participate in adult education.

From a political perspective we can begin to understand the relationship of individuals to groups and to the larger society. An understanding of political ideologies can help us understand that many adults are interested in learning because they see education as a means of correcting social injustice and solving social problems. They view education not only as a means of gaining personally but also as a way toward organizing for collective action. Thus education is not only learning something, but it involves social change as well. The learning process, then, is a constant movement between reflection and action, what Freire (1970) calls praxis.

In summary, a synoptic philosophy reminds us to view the adult as learner from several perspectives—psychological, sociological, biological, historical, and political. From these various perspectives, we can begin to understand the adult learner as a more complete entity. We can also understand that the adult learner and learning are influenced by much more than what occurs in a classroom or a workshop, that many other factors influence what adults learn, how they learn, and their purposes for learning.

In reflecting on the case example presented at the beginning of this chapter, a synoptic analysis could help Mr. Ashley view the adult as learner from a broader perspective. Thus it could help Ashley understand adults in his community well beyond the limited information obtained from a needs-analysis survey.

To do synoptic analysis, one begins with the question: Where can I find information that will help me better understand something—in the example here, the adult learner? A basic guideline is to not be adversely influenced by one source of information—one discipline. To gain an understanding of the adult as learner, it is important to avoid being overly influenced by the psychologists, though recognizing the importance of what they have contributed.

Combining critical and synoptic philosophical techniques, we can gain an in-depth and critical understanding of the adult learner, but one important dimension is missing. What do we believe should be the view taken of the adult learner? This question leads us to the last phase of our analysis process, the normative analysis.

Normative Analysis

Let us think of an analysis of continuing education as a road map. A road map provides us with an assortment of destinations and an assortment of routes to these destinations. We can travel the interstate highways, usually a direct route. Or we can select a less-traveled road that may take longer but give us a more interesting trip. A good road map provides detail and includes alternatives and some information about these alternatives. The map, like critical and synoptic analysis, makes us aware of a variety of destinations and journeys we may select but does not tell us which destination we should seek or which road we should take to travel there.

By critically analyzing our view of the adult learner and by considering the variety of views presented to us by such disciplines as sociology, psychology, biology, and history, we can become confused. As continuing education practitioners, we are all concerned with the practical questions: After an analysis of the adult as learner, will I change my views? If I change my views about adults as learners, how will I translate this change into practice?

Normative analysis is concerned with such questions as: What view should I hold, and what practice should I follow that is consistent with that view? The basis for decision making is our basic beliefs, in this instance our basic beliefs about adults as learners. For example, some educators of adults hold the following beliefs about adults as learners:

1. Human life is special, and therefore human beings must be treated as human beings, not as head counts and bodies that fill empty chairs.
2. Every person should have equal opportunity to participate in educational offerings.

3. The ends do not justify the means. For instance, "huckster-ism" in recruiting cannot be condoned in the interest of maintaining student numbers.
4. Basic human rights must not be violated—the right to express oneself without threat of reprisal, the right to disagree with instructor and administrator, the right to fair treatment.
5. Quality must come before quantity. Educational programming must first focus on quality, then on promotion.
6. Learning is a value to be prized throughout a lifetime.

Getting in touch with our beliefs can be one of the most difficult tasks associated with normative analysis. We all have beliefs, but we usually have not thought much about them. Most of us have never written them down. Yet, it is the beliefs that we hold, both those we are aware of and those we are not aware of, that guide the practical decisions we make. Although it may sound strange, we are all driven in some measure by beliefs we do not know we have, as well as by those of which we are aware. Bem (1970) calls these unknown beliefs "zero-order beliefs." He says these are the beliefs which we take for granted and for which we know no alternative.

Becoming aware of our beliefs about adults as learners and then comparing our beliefs with our actions can be an unnerving experience. We may agree, at some level, with the belief "The ends do not justify the means," yet our promotional efforts to ensure enrollments may contradict that belief. The difficulty, once we have identified the contradiction, is to wrestle with the decision: Do we change our practice to accord with our beliefs? Do we change our beliefs to accord with our practice? Or do we accept the contradiction as a compromise that all of us must make from time to time?

We can also examine our beliefs at a level beyond simply becoming aware of them. We may say we believe that the ends do not justify the means, but how much is that belief really a part of us and not just a platitude? How committed are we to selecting action alternatives that truly reflect that belief?

These questions lead us to examine the uncomfortableness associated with change—attempts to change beliefs, attempts to bring practice into accord with identified beliefs. To recognize that a belief we have identified is one we want to abandon is a difficult decision. Change is usually difficult. If we recognize the inadequacy of a belief and have no alternative with which to replace it, or if we have several alternatives and cannot decide which one to accept, we have created a vacuum. Radical change in what we believe often occurs once we have identified certain beliefs with which we have become uncomfortable. We may experience a "paradigm shift." Ferguson (1980), drawing on Kuhn (1970), says that as we develop too many contradictions between our actions and beliefs, we eventually reach a crisis point. "A powerful new insight explains the apparent contradictions. It introduces a new principle . . . a new perspective" (p. 27).

Some readers may yet wonder why the normative analysis is necessary, particularly after collecting research from several disciplines. For instance, it would be reasonable to ask: Do we not know what action to take in educating adults once we have become acquainted with the sociological, the historical, the political, and particularly the psychological research about adults as learners? But, as John Dewey has pointed out, "It is for the sciences to say what generalizations are tenable about the world and what they specifically are. But when we ask what *sort* of permanent disposition of action toward the world the scientific disclosures exact of us, we raise a philosophic question" ([1934] 1969, p. 181). As educators of adults, we are interested in "what sort of permanent disposition of action" we wish to take toward adults as learners, based *not only on the scientific evidence we have available but also on the results of our systematic analysis.*

From the normative perspective, let us examine the Westwind situation introduced at the beginning of this chapter. In analyzing the case study we identified several assumptions about the adult as learner. The first assumption was that adult learners are participants. From a normative perspective, what action-related questions should we ask? (1) Should we, as educators of adults, encourage greater amounts of participation in our programs? (2) Should we try to bring into our classrooms and workshops those who have lower levels of formal schooling, including those who may be uncomfortable with formal settings? (3) Do we believe that participation is good, that it is the ideal toward which we should strive? (4) Do we recognize other approaches to learning that are as important? For instance, should we encourage more self-directed learning, realizing that many persons may learn better in nonsponsored educational settings than in our programs?

In analyzing the case study we identified two additional assumptions: Adults are consumers of knowledge, and the better we promote our programs, the more people will attend them. From the normative perspective we could ask: (1) Should knowledge be viewed as a commodity to be marketed? (2) Should we view the adult learner as a consumer of knowledge? (3) If not, what view should we hold? (4) If we reject the adult learner as consumer, what position do we take, as a representative of an agency or institution, in making known what we are offering? (5) How do we continue to exist when other agencies and institutions in the field continue to view the adult learner as consumer and accelerate their attempts at marketing and promotion? (6) How can we survive under these conditions? (7) Does not survival of providers include the necessity of competing for participants?

Later, in analyzing the case study, we examined what Professor Smith had said about continuing education students at Westwind College. His comments assumed that the adult learner tarnished Westwind's image. From a normative perspective, we then must ask: (1) What should be the image of a college or university? (2) Where does continuing education fit within this image?

These are the questions that normative analysis helps us make clear but does not answer. Each of us daily considers these questions as we work with colleagues, budgets, advisory committees, administrators, and our students. Thus analysis is an ongoing process that helps us see direction for, in this instance, understanding adults as learners. It does not give us quick prescriptive answers.

Summary

In this chapter we began to apply the framework for analyzing continuing education practice introduced in Chapter Two. The focus was on analyzing the adult as learner, applying principles of critical, synoptic, and normative analysis. By means of a case study, identifying and evaluating assumptions and raising basic questions about adults as learners were illustrated. Synoptic analysis emphasized the need to draw on information from fields beyond psychology in understanding the adult as learner. Normative analysis emphasized the importance of drawing on the results of critical and synoptic analysis for raising questions about new directions for one's practice.

6

Examining the Aims of Continuing Education

~~~~~~~~~~~~~~~~~~~~~~~~~~~~~~~~~~~~~~~

What do we mean by *aim*? It is a simple enough word; it means direction, purpose, or goal. In the context of continuing education, the title of this chapter means examining the purpose, goals, or direction of what we do and what our agency or institution does if we are employed by an agency or institution. But why bother with such an examination, one might very well ask. Are not the goals of agencies and institutions already established, so that there is little we can say about them? And if we are doing continuing education outside an agency or institution, do we not have more important things to do than examine aims? Are they not usually written to satisfy some governing board or some taxpayer group to prove that an agency or institution knows where it is headed, at least on paper?

These are all appropriate comments. But before we dismiss aims as unimportant, let us first acknowledge that the field of continuing education is filled with statements of aims. It is important that those of us who work in the field should understand the meaning of aims already written and widely distributed. And beyond understanding these aims, it would also seem important for us to be able to react to them. Do we agree or disagree with them?

Once we have done an analysis of the aims of continuing education that currently exist, then we may wish to go back to earlier questions: Why have aims? Who should develop aims for continuing education, and what are the issues involved when developing aims?

To begin this discussion, I would like to share a parable.

Maynard of Hidden Valley

Maynard was a frog who lived in Hidden Valley Pond. He and his fellow frogs had plenty to eat, the pond water was clean and pure, and life was generally easy and predictable.

The frogs in Hidden Valley Pond were industrious. One group of them gathered food day in and day out so all the frogs in the pond could eat well. Another group taught the little frogs how to swim, how to float on their backs, and how to sun on the lily pads. Another small group of frogs was called "Teachers of Older Frogs" (TOOFs). They taught the more mature frogs how to change jobs from, for example, little-frog teacher to food gatherer; and they taught older frogs how to keep up to date with their jobs. For instance, new ideas were always available on food storage techniques, so the TOOFs offered many workshops on "New Ideas in Food Storage." One of the most popular courses the TOOFs taught was "How to Adjust to Advanced Years."

The smallest group of frogs in the pond was the food storage frogs, those who collected the food from the food gatherers and dispensed it to all the frogs according to the amount and value of the frog work done.

The protector frogs were the most important frogs in the pond in the eyes of many. They were responsible for defending all frogs from the Great Blue Fish that roamed the pond and ate frogs if given an opportunity. Only last year ten frogs on a holiday had been eaten by the Great Blue Fish. After that tragedy, the frogs all agreed that more protector frogs were needed, and an increasing amount of food resources was allotted to the protector frog group.

Although all seemed to be going reasonably well, a major problem was developing. Owing to a thermal crack in the floor of Hidden Valley Pond, the water had slowly begun warming. The temperature rise was not noticed at first. All the frogs were too busy doing their jobs as little-frog teachers, food gatherers, and so on to concern themselves with something as unusual as the pond water warming. The temperature had risen many degrees before a few frogs began noticing.

Maynard Frog was a TOOF, a Teacher of Older Frogs. He was active in his local TOOF organization and had become a leader in the Hidden Valley Association of Teachers of Older Frogs (HVAOTOOF—pronounced "hava tough"). More outspoken than some frogs, Maynard was concerned early about the increasing temperature of the pond water. He had other concerns, too, many long-standing. He was not pleased with the young-frog teaching curriculum, he thought far too many food resources were going to the frog protectors, and he never understood why the food storage frogs had so much power in dispensing food. Sometimes Maynard raised questions about the purpose of TOOF activity. Most TOOFs agreed that they were far too busy to waste time thinking about something as abstract as purposes. Those who did want to consider purposes did not want to think beyond their own area of work. A few of the career-change TOOFs were willing to talk about the aims for that activity, and a few of the TOOFs who worked with retired frogs were willing to consider the direction for that activity. But almost none of the frogs thought they had any right to consider aims for TOOF activity beyond what they were trained to do.

Maynard continued raising questions. He had become very concerned about the increase in pond water temperature. No frog in the pond, as far as he knew, was doing anything about it. Perhaps the Blue Fish were worrying about the problem, but no one ever communicated with a Blue Fish. Finally, at a local TOOF meeting, Maynard announced: "The water in our pond is becoming too uncomfortable for swimming, for work, for doing anything."

His friends shook their heads, and one claimed, "Maynard, you're imagining things. The pond water is no different than it ever was. And if by chance it had become warmer, there's nothing we could do about it anyway."

Maynard gathered a few of his friends to talk about the problem, but none of them was enthusiastic about discussing the temperature of the pond water. So what if it was a little warmer? They were all adjusting, weren't they? And the frogs were so busy with their various tasks they had little time to worry about the pond water.

Each year the temperature of the water climbed a few more degrees. And each year the frogs continued as if nothing were happening. Some found they could not work as hard as before, but they blamed their advancing years for that.

Maynard Frog kept speaking out. "The pond water will soon be too hot for us to live in," he exclaimed. "What are we going to do about it? What alternative do we have? We should at least look at alternatives."

But fewer and fewer frogs even listened to Maynard. It took nearly all their energy just to keep up with their assigned tasks.

Some of the TOOFs resented what Maynard was doing. One of the most learned of the TOOFs, a teacher of teachers of older frogs, Professor I. Leopard, wrote an article for the *HVAOTOOF Quarterly* in which he said, "TOOFs should not become involved with questions where they have no expertise. Besides," this noted teacher of teachers wrote, "we have all we can do to meet the needs of our clientele, given the demographic trends showing a steadily increasing number of older frogs."

The article, of course, did not help Maynard's cause. His supporters dwindled to only a dozen or so. Finally, in desperation, Maynard quit his job and retired to a quiet little log in a backwater section of the pond. There he reflected on why his fellow TOOFs would not look beyond their areas of specialization. He particularly pondered why none of the frogs ever got concerned about the increasing temperature of the pond water.

Several months passed with little change in the pond temperature. On a clear, cool October morning, Maynard was the first frog to detect the slight tremor that shook the entire area that included Hidden Valley Pond. Maynard was on his way to inform his few remaining friends about what he thought was happening when the earthquake struck, allowing the pond water temperature to reach boiling in a matter of a few minutes.

Do you find yourself in the story? Does the story sound at all like your community? Do you have a Maynard in your agency or institution—are you Maynard? What can we learn from a frog story about the aims for continuing education?

1. Are there broad societal issues that continuing education should address? Why or why not?
2. Is it possible to address broad societal issues and at the same time carry on the day-to-day activities that most of us must do?
3. How do the aims for continuing education relate to the aims of other societal agencies and institutions, such as schooling, economic institutions, the military, and social welfare?
4. What influences the aims for continuing education?

These are some of the questions I will discuss in this chapter. But before doing so I would like to illustrate how one does a critical analysis of the aims of a continuing education agency. Following the critical analysis, I will illustrate one approach to synoptic analysis about aims followed by normative analysis in which the preceding and other questions will be discussed.

Critical Analysis

Following is a brief analysis of the aims of the Cooperative Extension Service (CES), taken from a 1983 Cooperative Extension document, *Extension in the '80s*. As most readers are aware, CES is one of the largest continuing education agencies in the United States, tracing back to federal legislation of 1914.

These are excerpts from the foreward to *Extension in the '80s*:

> The Cooperative Extension is a unique achievement in American education. It is an agency for change, a catalyst for individual and group action. . . .
> Cooperative Education is a vast partnership

made up of local residents, the state land-grant universities, the U.S. Department of Agriculture, and the county governments throughout the nation. All these groups share in planning, financing, and operating Extension programs.

Extension's job is education. The service transmits practical information produced by research centers and universities to the public. Extension's aim is to help people identify and solve problems, many times through the use of new technology.

Extension programs are designed to help fulfill local and state needs. Yet these programs are flexible enough to accommodate national objectives. More than 3,000 Cooperative Extension offices throughout the country form an information network that is nationally conceived, yet locally available. Extension's mission is better agriculture, better homes, better communities—in the aggregate, a better world [1983, p. 1].

Assumptions. What assumptions are inherent in this statement of aims, particularly as they apply to education? We note at least two dimensions: (1) statements of educational outcomes and (2) statements of approaches to reaching these outcomes. In the first category, we can identify the following assumptions:

1. The CES fulfills local and state needs and reflects national objectives.
2. Identifying and solving people's problems is a primary objective.
3. As a result of solving people's problems, local, state, and national objectives will be met.

We note the following assumptions about CES's approaches to accomplishing its aims:

1. Education means transmitting information to the public.

2. New technology can help people identify and solve problems.
3. The primary role of education in CES is problem solving.

Are these assumptions sound? What questions might we raise
about them?

1. Can we assume that solving individuals' problems will result in solving local, state, and national problems?
2. Will providing information to people give them what is
necessary to solve their problems?
3. In what way will technology help people identify and
solve problems? Is it possible that the technology on oc-
casion may itself be another problem for people?
4. Is education only a problem-solving activity?
5. Is education primarily the transmitting of information?

Metaphors. As stated in Chapter Three, metaphors are a
powerful way of communicating meaning. They give a name to
something that belongs to something else, they associate and
mix images, and in doing so they help to make communication
easier. But metaphors also carry with them particular kinds of
meanings. Without trying to be all-inclusive, let us identify a
few metaphors present in the CES mission statement.

In the first paragraph we find "catalyst for individual and
group action." The word *catalyst* is a metaphor, meaning, in its
root sense, altering of the speed of a chemical reaction caused
by an outside agent that itself does not change. This is a powerful metaphor because it suggests, again to be literal, that CES is
able to bring various people, problems, and information together and cause changes to occur. Of course one can question
whether any continuing education agency or institution can be
a catalyst in the true sense of the word, because agencies and institutions also change as the result of the programs they offer.
They are themselves often changed by bringing together people
and information.

A second metaphor is the "delivery system" metaphor
that has become fashionable in much of continuing education.

Phrases to suggest this metaphor are "The service transmits practical information" and "Extension offices throughout the country form an information network." The key words are "transmits" and "information network." We have earlier raised questions about the adequacy of an educational agency's definition of education when it suggests education is solely the transmitting of information, or to use the popular phrase, delivering information.

A third metaphor suggested is the benefactor metaphor. The statement includes such phrases as "Extension's aim is to help people" and "Extension programs are designed to help fulfill local and state needs." The benefactor metaphor is common in most if not all agencies and institutions of continuing education. The metaphor works on the assumption that people, communities, societies, business, and industry have problems and needs and that the particular educational agency or institution can "help" to meet the need or solve the problem. What is important to analyze in this metaphor is the deeper meanings of a helping relationship. Does a helping relationship imply a dependency relationship, the one helped depending on the helper for assistance? Does a helping relationship imply a paternalistic view, with some outside group knowing better what a person, group, or business ought to do? Does a helping relationship suggest that the one to be helped will take less than full charge of his or her own problem or need? These are some of the questions that require reflection before we endorse the benefactor metaphor.

Slogans. As stated in Chapter Three, slogans have been used often in continuing education, and they, like metaphors, have an important purpose. Slogans express and foster a community of spirit and provide a rallying cry for those who are members of the agency or institution, as well as providing a means of attracting new adherents. Let us examine two slogans embedded in the Extension mission statement: "It [Extension] is an agency for change" and "Extension's mission is better agriculture, better homes, better communities—in aggregate, a better world."

It is not atypical for slogans to sound good—in fact, to

sound so good that no one could possibly argue with them. This is true of these two slogans. Who can argue with "agency for change" or "better agriculture, homes, communities, and world"? But most slogans, when we begin to examine them, remind us of something greater than reality. Cooperative Extension slogans are no more overblown than the slogans of other educational agencies and institutions.

We can ask these questions about the slogans: Agency for changing what? Changing people—in what ways? Changing itself? Changing the direction of change? We could go on. As for the second slogan, we could ask, better than what? Than the present situation? What if some aspects of the present situation are already rather agreeable to the people close to it? Still change it? We could go on with similar questions. Embedded in this slogan is the assumption of progress, that society is constantly moving toward improvement. I will say more about this assumption later in this chapter.

Fundamental Questions. In addition to identifying assumptions, metaphors, and slogans about a statement of aims, we can ask fundamental questions about the aims. Such questions seek to go beneath the surface of the statements. They search for hidden meanings and also for value positions and ethical perspectives.

Let us look briefly at the Cooperative Extension statement of aims to see what fundamental questions might be raised. Cooperative Extension is a "partnership made up of local residents, the state land-grant universities, the U.S. Department of Agriculture, and the county governments throughout the nation. All these groups share in planning, financing, and operating Extension programs."

These are some questions that might be raised:

1. How is it possible to satisfy four different partners in deciding on educational programs: (a) local residents, (b) the university, (c) the Department of Agriculture (federal government), and (d) the county government?

2. To what extent do the educational programs become those supported by the elected and appointed government offi-

cials involved, not the programs desired by the "local residents"?

3. How is it possible to keep politics out of the programming decisions, particularly county and national politics? Is it important that politics be kept out?

4. What if the problem identified by the people is one that involves the county government officials? An example might be the level of social services available in a county. How does Cooperative Extension respond in this situation?

Let us examine another part of the statement: "The service transmits practical information produced by research centers and universities to the public."

1. Which information is transmitted? All? If not all, how are decisions made about what is transmitted? How is it decided which information is "good," which is "relevant," and which is "appropriate"? Who decides? Is some information of more value than other information? If so, who makes that decision?

2. Is education viewed solely as information transmission, as this statement implies?

3. What contribution does information make to solving problems and meeting needs of people and of communities? Some writers are questioning how much information actually contributes to problem solving. Agricultural writer Wendell Berry (1983) says, "The evidence is overwhelming that [information] does not solve 'the human problem.' Indeed, the evidence overwhelmingly suggests . . . that [information] is the problem" (pp. 48-52).

John Naisbitt (1982), author of *Megatrends,* writes: "We are drowning in information but starved for knowledge. . . . This level of information [the amount presently available to people] is clearly impossible to handle by present means. Uncontrolled and unorganized information is no longer a resource in an information society. Instead it becomes the enemy" (p. 24).

4. What ethical problems arise when certain information is

transmitted? During the late 1950s and 1960s some educational agencies, including CES, advocated the use of DDT in controlling barn flies and various plant pests. Little was known about the side effects of this insecticide, such as the effect it might have on the environment. Who is involved in making decisions from an ethical perspective about which information will be transmitted, and how are the various cautions communicated along with the information?

Synoptic Analysis

In the previous section I illustrated how to *critically* analyze aims of continuing education. In this section I illustrate how to do a *synoptic* analysis of aims. As explained earlier, synoptic analysis examines phenomena broadly. One way to examine aims for continuing education is from a historical perspective.

Continuing education activities can be traced to preliterate times, when culture was transmitted from one generation to another. But as historian C. Hartley Grattan (1955) points out, "It is not until we come to the Greeks that we have much to consider that directly bears upon adult education as it is thought of today" (p. 23).

The primary aim of Greek continuing education was to teach citizens how to lead the "good life." The Greeks had an extremely narrow definition of who were citizens, so the majority of Greek men and women were not touched by continuing education. The content of the Greek continuing education effort would today be classified as liberal arts; the curriculum focused on literature, drama, politics, and religion.

Preliterate, Greek, and other early continuing education efforts have some influence on present-day aims, but the last three centuries of continuing education have had a profound influence. In the 1700s in Great Britain, continuing education began as literacy education. Its aim was "to teach poor working people of all ages to read and understand the Bible and the Catechism. . . . The larger object was always to save the poor in religious and moral terms. . . . There was no thought of training the pupils for citizenship, for the poor then had no citizenship in our modern sense; nor of developing their faculties in general, for it was feared that that would declass them" (Grattan, 1955, p. 65). Other forms of continuing education developed in Great Britain. One interesting continuing education movement became known as societies for moral improvement. These societies, operating in the middle 1700s, had a variety of aims. "Many of them became societies for religious improvement, while others directed their whole attention to the suppression of vice by entreating and exhorting offenders to abandon their evil courses, and by punishing great numbers, they, by slow, yet sure means, effected a visible improvement in the public morals" (Hudson [1851] 1969, p. 28).

In the early 1800s, mechanics' institutes began developing in Great Britain. They spread to several Commonwealth countries and to the United States. The mechanics' institutes had essentially three aims: "they should promote a knowledge of general science, diffuse rational information to the workers, and elevate character by providing worthwhile 'intellectual pleasures' and 'refined amusements.' They tried to teach workers the scientific principles *behind* their vocational practices, not the vocations themselves" (Grattan, p. 84).

Early continuing education in colonial America had a primary aim to assist people in reading the Bible and gaining salvation. This was also the aim of the common, tax-supported school organized for young people. After the American Revolution, citizenship training, trade knowledge, and information about science began replacing religious aims.

Benjamin Franklin's Junto, organized in 1727, was a forerunner of a broader approach to continuing education than literacy and religious education. Discussed at Junto sessions were such topics as politics, natural philosophy, and applied matters such as business techniques, practical medicine, and mechanical arts.

But religious aims for some continuing education institutions remained for many years. The Chautauqua movement was a prominent example. The Reverend John Vincent is given primary credit for organizing the Chautauqua, which had its first meeting in 1874. A project of the Methodist Episcopal church, the early Chautauqua had religious roots but soon included many secular topics in its varied program. Vincent's aim for the Chautauqua was a universal liberal arts education for everyone. Vincent, in accord with Aristotle, believed that adults were better suited for in-depth discussion, reading, and reflection than children were.

The idea of universities offering public lectures goes back to the early 1800s. A Rutgers professor offered public lectures on science in 1816. Professors from Harvard, Yale, Columbia, Michigan, Minnesota, and Wisconsin all offered lectures before 1890. But it was in the 1890s that an organized attempt to extend university resources to the community took hold. William Rainey Harper, while at the University of Chicago, is credited with being the first administrator to convince his faculty that the extension function should be equal to more traditional university functions.

Feeble at first, the idea of university extension slowly spread among the country's universities, particularly the state universities. At the University of Wisconsin in Madison, President Charles R. Van Hise, Governor Robert M. LaFollette, and Charles McCarthy of the Wisconsin Free Library Commission were instrumental in promoting "the Wisconsin idea," an interesting connection between the university and state government (Carstensen, 1981, pp. 7-13). President Van Hise, in his 1903 inaugural address, suggested university professors make themselves available as technical experts to state government. Nearly fifty professors were serving as technical consultants to state government by 1912 (Shannon and Schoenfeld, 1965, pp. 13-14). Thus a further aim of this early University of Wisconsin Extension was to help draft state policy in addition to making university resources available to the citizens of the state.

Lincoln Steffens, when assessing the continuing education role of the University of Wisconsin, said, "The University of Wisconsin is as close to the intelligent farmer as his pigpen or his toolhouse. The university laboratories are a part of the alert manufacturer's plant. To the worker the university is drawing nearer than the school around the corner and is as much his as his union is his. Creeping into the minds of his children with pure seeds; into the debates of youth with pure facts; into the opinions of voters with impersonal, expert knowledge, the state university is a part of the citizen's own mind" (quoted in Creese, 1941, pp. 53–54).

Cotton (1968) divided the aims of continuing education for the years 1919–1964 into three periods. Drawing on the works of such authors as Eduard Lindeman ([1926] 1961), Dorothy Canfield Fisher (1927), Everett Dean Martin (1932), and Basil Yeaxlee (1921), Cotton concluded that from 1919 to 1929 "adult education was seen primarily as an instrument for bringing about social reform, social reconstruction, and social progress—to realize the ideals of the 'good life' and the 'good society.' This 'idealistic' tradition represents a radical departure from the orientation of continuing education before World War I, with its emphasis on making up the educational deficiencies of adults" (1968, p. 4).

This interest in social change began to wane by the early 1930s. Adult educator Lyman Bryson wrote: "An old human impulse reorganized with a new name—and that is what a movement usually amounts to—suffers from the demand that it shall save the world. Adult education is not escaping this embarrassment. Enthusiasts are trying to make of it a remedy for all social and intellectual ills. The desire to make it a cure-all [is] certain to end in disappointment. The reaction will come when it is discovered once again that, even with the aid of this latest magic, painful and lengthy labors are needed to bring meager results" (1931, p. 161). Bryson's statement was symbolic of the move to a more "professional view" of continuing education. This new view emphasized continuing education's concern for the intellect, for ideas, for information and the use of information to solve problems. Rejected was the idea that continuing education should be involved in social reform and partisan politics.

The second period Cotton (1968) describes is 1930–1946. Affected greatly by the Depression and then World War II, the aims of continuing education continued to move from primarily social reform "to that of a more purely educational undertaking—toward the recognition of adult education as a fourth level of education" (p. 9). During these years, continuing education aims included (1) assisting with social and economic reconstruction (veteran training programs were an example), (2) helping people adjust to a rapidly changing society, (3) assisting people with problems related to technology, (4) providing literacy education, and (5) providing outlets for people's creative interests. Cotton (1968) says, "The 1930s stand as a transitional phase in the evolution of the movement. It was a period during which the *idea* of adult education became more established on the American scene, even if the *practice* of that idea was somewhat difficult to put into effect" (p. 10).

The third period Cotton mentions, 1947–1964, saw continuing education move more toward becoming a profession with professional adult educators. During this time the aims of continuing education included most of those mentioned for the previous period, with considerably less emphasis on social and economic reconstruction toward the end of the period.

The period 1964 to the present suggests further shifts in aims.

Aims: 1964 to the Present

Since 1964 many changes have occurred in continuing education, with effects on stated aims. The variety of providers was somewhat limited before 1964; colleges and universities offered much of the continuing education available. From 1964 to the present, many additional providers came on the scene. Prominent in the group were business and industry, whose continuing education activities have become the fastest-growing segment of the field. Also prominent at this writing are the continuing education opportunities offered by libraries, museums, labor organizations, political parties, neighborhood groups, private consulting firms, churches, health organizations, Boy Scouts, Girl Scouts, YMCA and YWCA, and a host of others. Of course universities, community colleges, and vocational/technical centers continue to expand their continuing education opportunities.

The aims for these varied providers help us understand the direction the field has taken during the past twenty years.

Continuing Professional Education. Improving the competence and performance of professionals such as medical doctors, attorneys, nurses, occupational therapists, dentists, and public school teachers became a dominant aim for much of the field. Houle (1980, p. 7) summarizes this development: "Because earlier, less formal means of learning did not suffice, the concept of 'continuing professional education' evolved, and the term itself came into general usage late in the 1960s. Initially it was restricted to only a few devices and techniques, the most common of which were the short course, lecture series, or conference, often housed in a residential setting. Gradually, however, the concept broadened to include all efforts to provide learning for active professionals." Some states passed legislation mandating that certain professionals participate in continuing professional education. Likewise, some professional organizations required continuing professional education for continued membership.

Career Development Education. Continuing professional education is one type of career development education. During the 1960s and 1970s and into the 1980s, career development as an aim was defined broadly to include all types of careers, not only those related to the professions. In a study conducted by the Future Directions of a Learning Society project of the College Board, 83 percent of adult learners sampled named some change or transition in their lives as a motivation to start learning. About half said changes in their jobs had motivated their return to education—they needed to learn to get a job, to get a better job, to keep the job they had, or to advance in their job (Aslanian and Brickell, 1980).

Also during these years, large numbers of men and women began to return to college and university classrooms to begin degree programs or to complete degree programs interrupted by marriage, jobs, economic conditions, war, or a variety of other factors. A majority of the returning students were women. On some community college campuses as many as 50 percent of students were twenty-five or older. Even at the large university research campuses, increasing numbers of older students were in attendance, often more than 30 percent of the student body.

Remedial Adult Education. A third segment of continuing education that gained prominence in the 1960s and 1970s was education with the aim of correcting inadequacy. Federal legislation such as the Manpower and Development Act of 1962, the Vocational Education Act of 1963, the Economic Opportunity Act of 1964, and the Adult Education Act of 1966 greatly expanded programs for Americans with "educational inadequacy." The Economic Opportunity Act of 1962, the so-called War on Poverty, provided money to establish extensive Adult Basic Education programs (ABE) throughout the country. An "Adult Performance Level" study funded by the U.S. Office of Education reported the following in 1975: "One out of five—19.8 percent—American adults . . . lacks the skills and knowledge needed to function effectively, and another 33.9 percent are marginally competent. . . . Only about 46.3 percent of us . . . are functioning with any degree of real competence. . . . five general knowledge areas [are] necessary [for] adult competence: occupational knowledge, consumer economics, government and law, health, and community resources" (Roth, 1976, p. 6).

Education for Personal Development. How to improve oneself as a person, how to maintain good physical and mental health, and how to develop personal skills such as writing or speaking are examples of aims related to personal development.

During the 1960s and 1970s several researchers reported on the various experiences and challenges that adults face as they age. Considerable research along these lines had been done with children and youth but little with adults. Bromley (1966) classified all of human life into sixteen stages from conception to senescence. Havighurst (1972) divided the life span into six age periods and described what he called developmental tasks for each life period. Erikson (1963) proposed eight ages of a person's ego development. Sheehy (1976) wrote about passages in human life, and Levinson (1978) researched characteristics of men's lives. Knox (1977) reviewed research on adult development and related it to adult learning. From such research and writing, much of it in the popular press, many educational programs were spawned. How to meet the challenges of the various ages and stages more satisfactorily and how to meet the challenges of midlife became themes for continuing education programming.

Beginning in the 1960s, the idea of self-directed learning has gained considerable prominence. One could improve oneself by oneself. Tough (1971) reported that more than 70 percent of the learning projects participated in by adults were self-directed. Knowles (1975) wrote a little how-to book illustrating how learners can take charge of their own learning, and Smith (1982) developed in considerable depth the idea of learning how to learn.

In addition, many continuing education providers focused on education "for coping with change." With the tremendous technological changes during these decades, culminating in the late 1970s and the 1980s with microcomputers and robots (the "steel-collar worker"), adults flocked to workshops and conferences to learn how to cope.

A persisting aim for some continuing education programs, particularly those of colleges and universities, was liberal arts education for adults. Programming in the liberal arts area, though never as popular as career development education or education for coping, continued as a small yet important programming segment. The area of liberal arts education for adults is the development of the person through examining accumulated ideas and truths from the arts, sciences, and humanities. These ideas and truths are constantly examined from the perspective of present-day human experience, particularly from the viewpoint of the person involved in the examination. The aim of liberal arts education includes, as adult educator John Hostler (1981) indicates, "seeking to make people more aware of their own character and potential, of their social background and conditioning, of the possibility of alternative values, and of the very nature of right and wrong . . . [liberal arts education] is trying to enhance tolerance, insight and integrity, and other aspects of what might be called . . . 'moral maturity' . . . the phrase implies that [adults] know what it is to be a moral agent: it means that they accept the necessity of choosing values, that they are conscious of the difficulties of applying them in practice, and that they are trying to grow towards their own ideal of life" (p. 37).

Educational philosopher R. W. K. Paterson (1979) expressed the aims of liberal arts programming this way: "Educational activity [in the liberal arts] is one which fosters the highest development of individuals as persons, and that the development of persons essentially consists in the enlargement of *awareness*. . . . To foster the development of the adult as a person, then, to educate him, is to extend the scope and enrich the quality of his awareness, and when we deem an activity to be educational in character, we do so by virtue of its pursuit and achievement of this governing principle" (p. 67).

Cultural Criticism and Social Change. Two broad movements can be identified for continuing education with aims for cultural criticism and social change from 1964 to the present: (1) the community development movement and (2) the radical adult education movement.

Examples of continuing education activity with community development aims include programs sponsored by Cooperative Extension and those generated by the Economic Opportunity Act of 1966. The aims of Cooperative Extension community development focused generally on rural problems—rural zoning, farm land preservation, and increasing nonfarm employment opportunities in rural communities. Economic Opportunity-sponsored community development focused on problems of the poor: inadequate housing, sanitation problems, problems faced by the elderly, and increasing skills for participation in community problem solving. These are but two examples of continuing education with community development aims. Other examples include community development sponsored by neighborhood organizations, public schools, and churches.

Radical adult education (Elias and Merriam, 1980) includes the activities of Saul Alinsky (1971) and social change programs in Chicago, Miles Horton's work at Highlander (Adams, 1975), Paulo Freire's literacy work (1970), and John Ohliger's (1974, 1975) work with Basic Choices. These efforts generally had aims of both cultural criticism and social change. Whereas community development activities generally fit within the existing social and economic structure in a community, radical adult education efforts often begin by challenging the existing institutions and structures. Although the examples just cited have been notable, continuing education activities with aims for cultural criticism and social change have been minor compared with the number of career-related or remedial adult education programs.

In summary, over the years the aims for continuing education have included—

1. Personal development, including the development of personal skills and liberal arts education.
2. Remedial education—correcting shortcomings of an adult's previous formal schooling as well as providing English as a second language and related immigrant education programs.
3. Religious education—much early adult education in England and the United States had religious aims.
4. Cultural criticism and social action education. Education for social change was a prominent aim for continuing education particularly in the 1920s. Societal attention to this aim continues in the 1980s, primarily in the area of community development. Cultural criticism as an aim has received little attention since the 1920s.
5. Education for career development—an aim for continuing education for many years. This has become the most prominent aim, particularly if continuing professional education is included within it.

Normative Analysis

In this section we will examine several questions: What should be the aims of continuing education, and who should decide what they ought to be? What forces influence aims for continuing education? Where do practitioners fit into the decision-making process of determining aims? At what level are aims determined for the field: At the agency or institution level? At some more global level that is broader than any single agency or institution? How do we consider aims for the field that transcend agencies and institutions—that relate to self-directed learning, for example?

Recall the questions mentioned earlier in the chapter. Should continuing education aims relate to broad societal issues? How do aims of continuing education relate to aims of other agencies and institutions in our society?

The pressures and challenges of our day-to-day work leave continuing education practitioners with little time or energy to consider aims. In addition to such pressures that steal time from considering aims, other factors that influence aims in continuing education include (1) society's dominant paradigm, (2) client influences, and (3) political pressures.

Society's Dominant Paradigm. The dominant paradigm— the beliefs, values, and assumptions that people in a society hold—greatly influences what happens in that society. The dominant paradigm is so ingrained in people that they often are not aware that they subscribe to it. When people are not aware of the dominant paradigm, they see no possible alternative to it.

One of the elements of the dominant paradigm that now influences aims for the field is the importance of specialization. Every aspect of society has become increasingly specialized, from health services to home repair. As noted in the parable of Maynard of Hidden Valley, people in a society have tasks to do, but they seldom know or are much interested in the tasks of others. As philosopher Mortimer Adler (1982) writes, "We need specialists for our economic prosperity, for our national welfare and security, for continued progress in all the arts and sciences, and in all fields of scholarship" (p. 72).

But the influence of specialization in Western culture has gone well beyond specialization in jobs and societal functions. Geographer Yi-Fu Tuan (1982) points out that an outcome of specialization is individualism. "Individualism, self, and self-consciousness—these and other related concepts are supremely the products of Western culture. In the West, the self has grown apart from others in prideful and nervous sufficiency. We are islands, each a world of its own; or, to use Goethe's metaphor, billiard balls, hard individuated objects that touch each other only at the surface" (p. 151).

Along with the rest of society, continuing education's aims have become specialized. As pointed out earlier in this chapter, a major aim of present-day continuing education is career development education. Usually this means specific and highly specialized education for career areas such as teaching, law, medicine, computer science, and business management.

Some people are questioning the extreme emphasis on specialization in this society's dominant paradigm. For instance, Adler says, "We can and should do something to mitigate the barbarism of intense specialization, which threatens to be as destructive in its own way as the abandonment of specialization would be" (p. 72). Capra (1983) says we have a crisis of ideas in this country. "The real problem that underlies our crisis of ideas [is] that most academics subscribe to narrow perceptions of reality which are inadequate for dealing with the major problems of our time. These problems . . . are systemic problems, which means they are closely interconnected and interdependent. They cannot be understood within the fragmented methodology characteristic of our academic disciplines and government agencies" (p. 25). Despite its critics, however, specialization continues to be an important feature of society's dominant paradigm.

A second element of our current paradigm is its emphasis on efficiency. "Do more with less" and "Do more in less time" are slogans in our society these days. Coming out of the industrial revolution, when the phrase "Time is money" was coined, the ideal of efficiency continues to influence all of our society, including the aims for continuing education. Adult educator Robert Carlson (1972) writes, "Virtually all the seminal ideas adopted by adult educators in recent years have resulted from empirical searches for more efficient ways to expedite learning. Carl Rogers advocated the encounter group. Ralph Tyler and Jerome Bruner promoted conceptual learning. Benjamin Bloom pressed for careful delineation of behavioral objectives. Malcolm Knowles sought to create the 'educative community.' And B. F.

Skinner argued that his operant conditioning was a more efficient method of achieving learning than any of the others" (p. 320).

An assumption of the importance of efficiency affects continuing education at many levels these days. With tight budgets, we hear, perhaps too often, that "we must get more bang for the buck," meaning that somehow education can be viewed as input (dollars) equaling output (education). One problem with this equation is coming to an agreement on exactly what the output is. A further, more important problem is the belief that one can always think of education in a direct cause-and-effect fashion: So many dollars inserted equals so much education in return. This is not to say that educators should not be accountable for budgets. Indeed they should be. But there are problems with using an efficiency model to describe and explain educational activity at any level.

Yet another assumption in the dominant paradigm is that the scientific method is the only valid approach to knowledge. Corollary assumptions are that science generates new technology and that new technology is good. Many writers are questioning these assumptions, though not denying that they continue to be driving forces in our society. Cavalieri (1981) writes: "There are numerous fundamental flaws in the entire scientific enterprise and its associated technologies. In many important instances science has become subservient to technology, which in our society is tuned to boundless growth and expansion. Ideally, science should be independent of this influence but not of human or societal needs. A real concern for these needs would require a serious evaluation of research efforts leading to long-range planning of the scientific enterprise and careful advance assessment of the applications of science, conditions that do not obtain at present. . . . More and more frequently we are faced with problems created by 'solutions' to the problems arising from previous technologies. For example, increasing food production by the use of more fertilizer leads to water pollution. . . . What we are witnessing in general are the results of a technocratic system that lacks a self-correcting servomechanism; there are no built-in provisions for monitoring new developments in different fields and adjusting them in order to optimize the well-being of society as a whole" (pp. 16, 20).

Other writers agree that the scientific method alone cannot provide the breadth of answers and information that humankind requires. Ferguson (1980, p. 48) says, "We were naive in our expectation that mechanistic science would explain the mysteries of life." A narrow emphasis on the scientific method excludes the contributions of history, of philosophy, of the arts and humanities to understanding and perspective. An all-encompassing reliance on the scientific method to provide answers and to advance knowledge relegates the arts and humanities to entertainment. Arts and humanities are viewed as interesting diversions to a busy life but not as providing anything fundamental to humankind.

Herein lies the important influence of the scientific method on the direction of aims in education. With sole reliance on the scientific method, education as a process is viewed as incremental and linear. Information obtained builds on further information, in a never-ending accumulation process. One aim of education, then, becomes the continuing accumulation of information. And perhaps even more important, this view of education often excludes the importance of value systems.

Richard Wear (1977) calls those who subscribe to the scientific/technological approach to education the "New Carthaginians." Wear writes: "It is not the sometimes hazardous or wasteful creations of our New Carthaginians, or even the occasionally pernicious by-products of their efforts, that should provoke our opposition, but the failure of education to sufficiently encourage bright young minds to develop personal value systems predicated on something more substantial than whim and expedience. ... there must be room in every curriculum for those courses that will inspire students to think of people before goals, values before dollars, and perhaps even the spirit before the flesh" (p. 32).

Another assumption in our society's dominant paradigm is that the ultimate purpose of education is for career. This assumption has become prevalent during the last ten years. Few would deny that education does relate to career in many important instances. But during the past two decades, education has become increasingly tied to vocation, at every level from elementary education through various applications of continuing education.

The dangers related to the assumption that education is for career are many. Humanist Raymond Dennehy (1982) relates: "The failure of vocationalism is that it can produce only mere specialists. Unlike the educated person, the mere specialist knows only those principles that pertain to his specific area of expertise. He thus erroneously supposes either that all areas of human endeavor are areas of technical specialization with the consequence that he is quite content to leave the task of governing in the hands of those whose expertise governing is or, because he views and judges all reality from the standpoint of the narrow, specified principles of his specialty, he will be inclined to evaluate all of human experience on their basis. The first alternative begets exactly what the vocationalists seek to avoid —elitism. For if the people demonstrate their incompetence for self-rule, then we shall have a ruling class of either the paternalistic or totalitarian stamp" (pp. 191–192). But regardless of the failures of a narrow view of vocationalism and its dangers to society, the majority of continuing education programs are related in one way or another to job and career.

Writers like Mortimer Adler (1982) describe the need for a balanced set of aims for education. When discussing college and university education, Adler says that preparation for vocation "that requires specialized knowledge and technical training" (p. 70) should be one purpose, but a second important one is a "pursuit of general learning itself" (p. 71). By *general learning* Adler refers to acquisition of knowledge in such broad areas as language, literature, and the fine arts; mathematics and natural sciences; and history, geography, and social sciences (pp. 22–24). In continuing education today, far more attention is paid to education related to career than to what Adler calls "general education."

Other elements of the dominant paradigm we could list include accumulation of material goods as a sign of success, the importance of success for individual well-being, and an assumption that time is linear and that change is incremental. Alvin Toffler (1980) reminds us that "many preindustrial societies [saw] time as a circle, not a straight line. From the Mayas to the Buddhists and the Hindus, time was circular and repetitive, history repeating itself endlessly, lives perhaps reliving themselves through reincarnation" (p. 95). From an assumption of time as linear, it follows that change is viewed as additive—that each new research finding, for example, builds on a previous one.

Further elements of the dominant paradigm include (1) an assumption that all change is the result of some identifiable and measurable outside force and (2) a belief that society is a collection of individuals pursuing their own interests and that the function of institutions and government is to enhance this purpose for individuals.

All these elements of the dominant paradigm influence the aims of continuing education, as they influence all other elements of society. The influences are expressed in a variety of ways. For instance, extension administrator Phillip Frandson (1979) described the pressure groups that he saw influencing the aims for college and university continuing education. He saw two major categories of constituencies influencing aims: those within the institution and those in the outside community. Frandson pointed out, "Facing a decline in enrollment-based funding, administrative units are suddenly turning their attention to the substantial fee income currently enjoyed by extension and continuing education divisions" (p. 12). And consequently units that have not been involved with or particularly interested in continuing education activities in the past now want to become involved and have something to say about the aims and direction for continuing education programs.

Frandson raises a series of questions concerning influences from outside the university and their role in dictating aims for continuing education programming: "Who shall set the standards for the content, format, and methodologies for [programs in continuing education for the professions and other career areas?] Who shall plan, develop, and present specific courses and sequential curricula? Who shall determine whether or not relicensure should be required in any given profession?" (p. 12).

Frandson succinctly outlines these many pressures that influence the aims of continuing education in higher education institutions. Similar pressures influence other continuing education agencies and institutions. Reflection on the dominant paradigm assumptions just outlined above shows that these so-called practical influences on aims are really manifestations of the influence of the dominant paradigm. They are, in effect, examples of how the dominant paradigm works in our society.

Several questions can be raised: How prevalent is the dominant paradigm? How should adult educators respond to the dominant paradigm? To what extent can the aims for continuing education influence the direction of a dominant paradigm? These are the questions we will explore in the next section.

Changing Times. Naisbitt (1982), Toffler (1980), Ferguson (1980), and others point out that the dominant paradigm as I have described it is not as dominant as it once was. In many parts of the world, including the United States, people are experiencing a paradigm shift. New values and beliefs are emerging; old ones are questioned and modified or ignored. For example, increasingly, scientific proof is questioned as the only way toward understanding, a linear view of time is questioned, and rationality is challenged as the sole approach to thought. "Western society is at a pivotal point. Many key thinkers have had the paradigm shift about how paradigm shifts happen, a revolution in understanding how revolutions begin: in the ferment of questions, in the quiet recognition that the old won't do" (Ferguson, 1980, p. 37).

These changes will influence the aims for continuing education. The important question, it seems, is whether the field of continuing education wishes to continue to respond to changes in society, as it has for the past four decades. Will aims for continuing education change in response to societal changes? Or will continuing education take advantage of what some are calling "a rare moment in history" for education and become proactive—that is, begin to influence the direction in which society is going?

Let us assume for a moment that shaping the direction for society is an appropriate aim for continuing education. What might we do as adult educators to implement that aim? We could conduct educational activities that allow participants to examine and challenge the assumptions of present-day society. Such educational activities could focus on such practical concerns as unemployment, leading to a discussion of the nature of work in present-day society and the likely future of work. Educational activities could focus on the problems in schooling, examining the nature of education, its assumptions, and what its goals ought to be. Out of such discussions would come a challenge to our present assumptions about society—for example, our assumptions about work and about schooling.

Once the assumptions are challenged—and this is an extremely important first step and one reluctantly acccomplished because many people are so accepting of the dominant paradigm that they see no need to challenge—we can begin to frame new questions. As Ferguson (1980) explains when describing how to work toward paradigm shifts, "We do this by asking questions in a new way—by challenging our old assumptions . . . most problems cannot be solved at the level at which they are asked. They must be reframed, put into a larger context. And unwarranted assumptions must be dropped" (p. 28).

What Aims for Continuing Education? Continuing education will continue to have as its aims (1) education for career development, including improving the competence and performance of professions through continuing professional education activities, (2) remedial education to correct the inadequacy of previous schooling or to teach English as a second language, and (3) education for personal development.

Cultural criticism leading toward social change should become a more prominent aim than during the past several decades. Society is changing; basic assumptions are being challenged and replaced. Do we as adult educators want to be a part of that activity, or do we wish to sit by, watching it occur and waiting for the changes so we can then adapt our adult education programming accordingly? Is it time for continuing education to become more proactive, as it was during the 1920s?

Summary

In this chapter I have discussed aims for continuing education from three broad perspectives: (1) critical analysis—examining assumptions, metaphors, and slogans; (2) synoptic analysis—examining the broad sweep of aims for the field from a historical perspective; and (3) normative analysis—examining the future of aims for the field, with a focus on what influences aims.

Using a statement of aims from a continuing education agency document, I illustrated how to identify and raise questions about assumptions, about metaphors, and about slogans. I also presented several examples of fundamental questions that could be raised about the statements of aims presented in the agency document.

I traced the development of aims for the field from earliest times to the present, showing how aims have changed over the years.

In the normative section, I showed how the dominant paradigm in society has influenced aims for continuing education. The dominant paradigm is shifting, and we need to consider what role continuing education would like to have during this process of change.

Consideration of aims is not only a topic for a handful of adult educators in high-level leadership positions but a topic for all of us who work in the field. What is the aim of what we do, and what should be the aim of what we do, are questions we should never cease asking.

7

Reconsidering Current Teaching and Learning Approaches

∿∿∿∿∿∿∿∿∿∿∿∿∿∿∿∿∿∿∿∿∿∿

In recent years more has been written about how to teach adults and how adults learn than about any other topic in continuing education. This is understandable. The field includes many practitioners who are concerned about how to better teach adults. And of course, anyone interested in improving teaching is also interested in the characteristics of the adult as learner, how adults learn, and what influences their learning.

In the literature of teaching and learning in continuing education, it is easy to find considerable diversity of opinion. Educators of adults do not agree on the best approach for teaching adults; indeed, they do not agree on how adults learn. This is typical for much of education, from preschool to graduate education.

In this chapter I will examine teaching and learning in continuing education from several perspectives. First, following the tenets of critical analysis described earlier, I will analyze two statements representing quite different positions on teaching and learning. In the synoptic analysis section of this chapter, I will examine teaching and learning from several perspectives that are prominent in the literature today. Then, in the norma-

131

tive analysis section, I will look at several shortcomings of present practices in teaching and learning and suggest alternative approaches.

Critical Analysis

Following are excerpts from two books that have been widely used in continuing education as well as in other educational applications. I will first introduce the excerpts and then list assumptions about each of them. First excerpt: "Once an instructor decides he will teach his students something, several kinds of activity are necessary on his part if he is to succeed. He must first decide upon the goals he intends to reach at the end of his course or program. He must then select procedures, content, and methods that are relevant to the objectives; cause the student to interact with appropriate subject matter in accordance with principles of learning; and, finally, measure or *evaluate* the student's performance *according to the objectives or goals* originally selected" (Mager, 1962, p. 1).

What assumptions can be identified?

1. The teacher has complete control of the learning situation, including what the student will learn and how.
2. Teaching is sequential; there is a definite beginning and ending to teaching activity.
3. It is possible to predict the outcomes of a teaching activity.
4. It is possible to measure the outcomes of a teaching activity in terms of student performance.
5. What students learn is external to them.
6. Learning means interacting with appropriate subject matter.
7. Students must be able to perform something as an indicator that learning has occurred.

Second excerpt: "I have come to feel that the only learning which significantly influences behavior is self-discovered, self-appropriated learning. Such self-discovered learning, truth that has been personally appropriated and assimilated in experience, cannot be directly communicated to another. As soon as an individual tries to communicate such experience directly, often with a quite natural enthusiasm, it becomes teaching, and its results are inconsequential. . . . When I try to teach, as I do sometimes, I am appalled by the results, which seem a little more than inconsequential, because sometimes the teaching appears to succeed. When this happens I find that the results are damaging" (Rogers, 1969, p. 153).

Assumptions related to this passage include the following:

1. Teaching is an overrated activity.
2. Teaching usually interferes with learning.
3. Learning that is most important to a person is not the result of teaching; it is self-discovered.
4. It is impossible to communicate what one has learned directly to another person.

Let us compare the two sets of assumptions and also the two statements. Those who have worked in continuing education for any length of time recognize the two statements as representing polar positions held by many adult educators. On the one hand are the behaviorists, represented by the first passage, and on the other are the humanists, represented by the second. When the assumptions are identified, it becomes more obvious why so much debate has developed between these two positions over the years.

The behaviorist position emphasizes a cause-and-effect relationship between teaching and learning. It suggests that if the teacher does certain things, then certain outcomes will result, which can be measured. The humanistic approach implicitly questions such a cause-and-effect relationship of teaching and learning; it suggests that teaching may indeed have outcomes quite different from what was intended and sometimes these outcomes may be negative. That is, teaching may sometimes be more harmful than useful.

A second distinction between the two positions concerns their views of learning. In the first passage, learning is viewed as accumulation of something that is external to the learner, and it can be expressed with some sort of learner performance. In the second passage, learning is much more of an internal activity and is specific to the learner. That is, two persons experiencing the same event will likely learn different things from it.

A third distinction relates to control. In the first passage, the teacher has considerable control over the learning situation and thus over the learner. In the second passage, the learner has the control and the teacher is in a secondary position. We could raise questions about the ethics of these relationships: Is it ethical for an educator of adults to have control over what an adult learns? But we could raise the opposite question as well: Is it ethical not to have control when adults pay fees to learn something and expect the learning to proceed in an organized, controlled fashion?

We could go on questioning and comparing these two positions about learning in adult education and even try to show how one view is better than the other. Indeed, this has been the approach taken by many educators of adults over the past several decades. I have myself taken this approach in one of my earlier books (Apps, 1979, pp. 150-173). No matter, both approaches remain prominent in continuing education and must be recognized. We might also question the validity of trying to show that one approach is superior in all instances. Is it possible that in some settings the two approaches could be merged and that something greater than either of them might emerge from the combination? Is it possible that a certain "hybrid vigor" might result from putting these two ideas about teaching and learning together into a new formulation that on the surface appears impossible because of the conflict in assumptions?

In this section I have illustrated how one of the approaches to critical analysis, identification of assumptions, can be used to gain insight into teaching and learning. I have picked an old argument about teaching and learning to make the point, but a dispute that is far from resolved. By selecting the example of behaviorist versus humanistic education, I do not mean to suggest that this is the most important issue facing teaching and learning, because it is not, in my judgment. In the normative section of this chapter I will explore other issues that I believe are of more import.

Synoptic Analysis

In a synoptic analysis, you will recall, one attempts to examine a topic from several perspectives. In the case of teaching and learning in continuing education, we are interested in what various disciplines can contribute to our understanding of this complex area. What follows is not in any way intended to be all-inclusive of the literature on teaching adults and adult learning. Rather, the intent is to show, by means of example, how one might begin doing a synoptic analysis of teaching and learning in continuing education. In this sample analysis, I will consider five perspectives: psychological, socioanthropological, technological, applied, and integrative.

Psychological Perspective. One strain of psychological research is concerned with changes in vision, hearing, and reaction time as a function of age and how these changes relate to adult learning (Bischof, 1976). Evidence shows, and any older adult will confirm, that one's vision and hearing does diminish with age, and ability to react slows down.

Another branch of psychological research has been concerned with adult intelligence and has addressed such questions as: Do some aspects of adult intelligence decline with age? Do other aspects remain constant or even increase? Researchers such as Bischof (1976), Wechsler (1972), Gilbert (1973), Baltes and Schaie (1974), Cattell (1963), Moenster (1972), Schaie and Parr (1981), and Schaie and Geiwitz (1982) have all addressed the question of adult intelligence in one way or another. Recent research in this area discusses two aspects of intelligence: fluid and crystallized. Crystallized intelligence reflects the skills adults acquire from formal education and from everyday living. It includes general information and the ability to perceive relationships based on acculturation, vocabulary, and arithmetic reasoning. Fluid intelligence includes short-term memory, verbal reasoning, and common word analogies. It is relatively independent of experience and education. Knox (1977, p. 464), in summarizing research in this area, says, "Performance on tests of fluid intelligence . . . tends to peak after adolescence and to decline gradually during adulthood. Performance on tests of crystallized intelligence . . . continues to increase gradually throughout most of adulthood. As fluid intelligence decreases and crystallized intelligence increases, general learning ability remains fairly stable" (p. 464).

Some of the early research, such as Thorndike's (1932), suggested that adults learned less well as they grew older. But Thorndike was concerned mainly with rate of learning. Declines in reaction speed and ability to hear and see do decrease the rate of learning somewhat. Today's researchers see the adult learning process as far more complex than a simple relationship of certain sensory functions to learning ability. For example, Knox (1977, pp. 410-411) cites seven modifiers of adult learning performance: (1) Condition—physical health, sensory impairment (eyesight, hearing, and so forth). (2) Adjustment—a personal and a social adjustment to the learning situation enhance learning performance. (3) Relevance—learning occurs more readily when the learning tasks are meaningful to the learner. (4) Speed—learning is enhanced when adult learners can proceed at their own pace. (5) Status—socioeconomic level and formal education are associated with adult learning. For instance, amount of formal education generally relates positively to participation in continuing education activities. (6) Age—older and younger adults may learn differently because of generational differences in experiences and values. (7) Outlook—degree of open- or closed-mindedness and personal outlook affect how adults face learning situations.

Psychologists such as Moenster (1972) have also been concerned with memory and how the ability to remember changes with age. "Research suggests some differences between that which is stored for immediate and short-term memory and that stored for intermediate and long-term memory. However, most memory testing for adults has been with immediate and short-term memory. The results of this research suggest that the ability to retain information in the immediate and the short-term memory declines very little throughout most of adulthood —if the material that has been encoded is meaningful, if it has been accurately encoded, and if the amount is not unreasonably large. Another conclusion of this research is that remembering information is easiest when the recall situation is similar to the situation where the registration of the material occurred" (Apps, 1981, pp. 91–92).

Educational psychologists have, over the years, devoted considerable time to the development of learning theories such as classical mental discipline, unfoldment, apperception, behaviorism, and Gestalt field. Much has been written about these theories (for example, Bigge, 1976), and considerable debate, like that illustrated at the beginning of this chapter, has taken place over which theory is the "correct" learning theory. These arguments continue, but as we shall see later in this chapter, some adult educators have taken a broader view of adult learning than what is inherent in these standard learning theories.

The educational psychologist Robert M. Gagné (1977) described learning as a series of steps:

1. Selective perception of a stimulus. Patterns of stimulation are perceived.
2. Short-term memory storage. Information is retained for a limited time, often only a few seconds.
3. Encoding. Information is transformed into a mode that has meaning for the learner and moves into long-term memory.
4. Storage. Information is stored in long-term memory.
5. Retrieval. Information is recalled from long-term memory, evidence that learning has indeed occurred.
6. Response. This includes how a person will respond to the learning in the form of speech, bodily movement, and so on, and the sequence and timing of the response.
7. Performance. As a result of the learning, a person displays patterns of activity that can be externally observed.
8. Feedback. The learner observes the effects of his or her performance and completes the "learning loop." This final step "provides the learner with the confirmation (or verification) that his learning has accomplished its purpose. . . . Although feedback usually requires a check which is external to the learner, its major effects are obviously internal ones, which serve to fix the learning, to make it permanently available. This is the phenomenon called *reinforcement*" (pp. 53–57).

Gagné (1977) has also described four broad categories of learning: (1) basic forms of learning, (2) discriminations, concrete concepts, (3) defined concepts and rules, and (4) problem solving—cognitive strategies. In the first category he describes signal learning, stimulus-response learning, chaining, and verbal association. These forms of learning range from a simple response to a noise, shock, or some other signal (signal learning) to putting together in new ways chains of language previously learned. Learning forms included in the second category are learning discriminations (how to differentiate responses to various stimuli) and learning concrete concepts (how to place information into classes and tell one class from another). In the third category Gagné has placed the learning of defined concepts and rules. "Many concepts cannot be learned . . . as concrete concepts. Instead, they must be learned by *definition* and, accordingly, may be called *defined concepts*" (p. 128). The various forms of learning in the fourth category, problem-solving learning, are in hierarchical order, from lower to higher forms. To perform problem-solving learning, a person must have mastered the forms of learning that precede it, particularly the application of previously learned rules.

In recent years developmental psychologists have researched adult development and have offered many useful insights. Some of the early work was done by Erik Erikson (1963), who identified developmental stages, and Robert Havighurst (1972), who identified developmental tasks. Neugarten (1977), Gould (1978), and Levinson (1978) also examined developmental stages as a focus of their research. Erikson (1963) proposed eight stages of psychosocial ego development. He suggested that one can be successful or unsuccessful during each stage of one's life. Erikson described three stages of adulthood: early, middle, and late. During early adulthood, he said, a person wrestles with intimacy and isolation. A capacity to commit self to others is intimacy. Isolation is avoidance of intimacy. In middle adulthood, one faces the tension between generativity and stagnation. Generativity is defined as being productive and creative for self and others, while stagnation means being egocentric and nonproductive. Resolving the tension between integrity and despair occurs during late adulthood. Acceptance of one's life is integrity, while despair means being overwhelmed by a sense of life failure and loss of faith in self and others (pp. 247-274).

Psychologists have given educators of adults much useful information. Yet, some educators depend almost entirely on the results of psychological research and writing without considering teaching and learning in continuing education viewed from other perspectives.

Some of the psychological study of adult learning can also be faulted for its mechanistic assumption. Gagné's work, cited earlier in this chapter, is an example. Gagné suggests that learning consists of a set of identifiable stages, although he recognizes that there may be several categories of learning. Psychologists such as Gagné have defined learning in a fairly narrow manner. Perhaps, for that learning in which one wishes to accumulate some new information for the purpose of some new performance, Gagné's and similar approaches make sense. For instance, a learner interested in developing word-processing skills may follow the Gagné model for learning. But what if the learner wants to develop an understanding of the moral issue of poverty or is concerned with appreciating rock music or perhaps identifying and doing something about community social problems? Does the Gagné model and others similar to it fit? Are there other perspectives that can help us better understand these learning situations and thus provide a different foundation for our roles as practitioners?

Socioanthropological Perspective. Anthropologists like Harry F. Wolcott (1982) who have examined teaching and learning in noninstitutional settings provide interesting perspectives. Wolcott says, "I have always been skeptical of social scientists or educators who regard teaching and learning as one and the same. I have also been uncomfortable with anthropological nonchalance in seeming to equate the *transmitting* of culture—particularly with self-conscious efforts within a society to do so—with the *learning* of culture" (1982, p. 83). Wolcott goes on to explain that anthropology has much more to offer education and educators than the method of ethnography—a fieldwork approach to research. Anthropology, according to Wolcott, can offer a new perspective to understanding learning in noninstitutional settings. Poking fun at the psychologists, Wolcott writes, "One gets little sense of awe or excitement in psychological treatises on the topic [of learning]. For most students, 'learning' is . . . dull and pedestrian . . . I still hear college students insist that all they need to know and all they want to know about learning is contained in the sterile definition 'a change in behavior.' Learning has become synonymous with classroom performance for pupils, sophomoric performance for sophomores, and maze performance for mice" (pp. 86-87). Wolcott goes on to say, "What a remarkable contribution anthropology could make to teaching if it could help teachers develop a proprietary interest in the natural (and very social) process of human learning and help educators shape a learning-centered rather than a teaching-centered profession" (p. 87).

Going beyond the actual learning process, several authors have discussed factors that influence learning. Tough (1971) has researched adults' natural tendencies toward learning (see the previous chapter). Smith (1982) has developed an approach to understanding how adults can learn how to learn more effectively.

Aslanian and Brickell (1980) have researched "triggers" that influence when people return to formal education. And in my own work (Apps, forthcoming) I have researched barriers to adult learning for adults who have returned to formal study. Juggling work time and school time, finding time with family, and the stress associated with these time demands were perceived by returning adult students as the greatest barriers to their learning.

From these and other writers it is possible to examine adult learning from a socioanthropological perspective and gain insights into factors that affect adult learning which go beyond the psychological dimension. As Simon (1969) points out, "Insofar as behavior is a function of learned technique rather than 'innate' characteristics of the human information-processing system, our knowledge of behavior must be regarded as sociological in nature rather than psychological—that is, as revealing what human beings in fact learn when they grow up in a particular social environment" (p. 76).

A synoptic analysis of socioanthropological literature about adult learning and factors related to it yields several suggestions for practitioners: (1) Help eliminate barriers to learning such as offering workshops at times that interfere with other learner responsibilities. (2) Develop a learning climate that reduces stress levels in learners. (3) Assist learners with learning projects they have identified (the educator is a guide and resource, rather than in control of what is learned). (4) Recognize that the learner's personal history influences his or her world view and may also influence the preferred learning style.

Technological Perspective. Technology, particularly the computer, affects how we view teaching and learning, probably more than most educators of adults would admit. Indeed, technology influences all of society in ways greater than most people know. For example, sociologist Daniel Bell (1980) writes, "In the coming century, the emergence of a new social framework based on telecommunications may be decisive for the way in which economic and social exchanges are conducted, the way knowledge is created and retrieved, and the character of the occupations and work in which [people] engage" (p. 163).

Educational technology is, of course, not new to continuing education. Radio, television, and telephone have long been allies for educators of adults. Now practitioners wrestle with how to fit computer applications into their educational programs. Carol Kasworm and Cheryl Anderson (1982) asked administrators of adult education programs how computers were used in their institutions. Nine categories of uses were reported:

1. Drill and practice—flashcard-type learning in adult basic education programs.
2. Tutorial—textual information is presented on the computer screen, with questions, and branches to different responses based on the answers given.
3. Problem solving—learners apply principles, rules, and the logic of science and math to solve problems.
4. Simulations—a model based on reality is presented that al-

lows learners to experience an approximation of their real-life decisions in a simulated environment.

5. Testing—criterion-based tests with questions generated at random are given to learners, with results immediately available.

6. Computer-managed instruction—learners are given a diagnostic test, and on the basis of the results, the computer provides a learning prescription. The learner may be directed to further computer-provided instruction or to other types of learning situations.

7. Information management—educators use the computer to manage budgets and keep records, inventories, and schedules.

8. Word processing—manipulation of reports, papers, and handouts.

9. Computer literacy--teaching adults about computers and how to use them (p. 91).

The question educators of adults often ask these days is "How can we make use of the computer in our educational programs?" Too often, though, the vision of computer use is too narrow, according to mathematics professor Seymour Papert (1980). He says, "Faced with a computer technology that opens the possibility of radically changing social life, our society has responded by consistently casting computers in a framework that favors the maintenance of the status quo" (p. 73).

Papert believes that the computer can have a revolutionary effect on all of education, from increasing the occurrence of self-directed learning through computers in the home to changing the relationship of student to teacher in the classroom. He recognizes that similar statements were made about the introduction of TV, film, and other educational technology in the classroom and that profound changes did not occur. But, Papert points out, "the computer can enter the educational process in a profoundly different way" (p. 80). Papert suggests that computer exercises can be developed that bring the learner "into a relationship with his own intuitive knowledge structures" (p. 83).

Because computers can handle vast amounts of information so efficiently, it is easy for educators of adults to see the computer as one more means of information transfer. By using computers in this manner, the adult educator is implicitly defining education very narrowly and not considering the vast potential for its use as both Bell and Papert have suggested. In the past, educators of adults have been trapped into believing they were educating when they use radio, telephone, and television to move information from one place to another. But the simple moving of information is not in itself education. The computer's vast potential for storage, organization, and retrieval of information makes it an even more attractive information-moving device than television, radio, and telephone. As David Gueulette (1982) argues, "Adult educators can and must influence the direction of . . . telecommunications. . . . The indication that education will increasingly become what the system can deliver is an ominous prospect and must be countered by educators who can develop content or curriculum specified by learner or societal needs" (p. 9).

Others, too, raise concerns about the so-called computer revolution we are experiencing. MIT computer science professor Joseph Weizenbaum (1980) says that one consequence of focusing on computers, which are touted as providing solutions for problems not yet identified, is to obscure persistent problems. Weizenbaum warns that computers will never and can never answer the deeper questions humankind faces. "Construction of reliable computer systems in the social and political sphere awaits not so much the results of research in computer science as a deeper theoretical understanding of the human condition. The limit, then, of the extent to which computers can help us deal with the world of human affairs is determined by the same thing that has always determined such limits: our ability to assess our situation honestly and our ability to know ourselves" (p. 453).

Other writers are even more critical of how computers are influencing humankind. Illich (1983) writes, "The machine-like behavior of people chained to electronics constitutes a degradation of their well-being and of their dignity which, for most people in the long run, becomes intolerable. Observations of the sickening effect of programmed environments show that people in them become indolent, impotent, narcissistic, and apolitical. The political process breaks down, because people cease to be able to *govern* themselves; they demand to be *managed"* (p. 5).

John Wicklein (1979) asks these broad questions:

> If we absorb information and entertainment, do our jobs, transact our business, and engage in personal interchange via the HCS [home communications set], how will this affect our social relationships? Will we become stay-at-homes, relating mostly to a machine, or will the interactions on the machine lead us into more personal contacts outside the home?
>
> Will the new communications collect information from the masses and funnel it to the few at the top, tending to centralize government and industry, or will it be a decentralizing force, providing more information to the populace so that more and better decision making can be done at the local levels?
>
> Will rich countries and multinational corporations use information extracted from the less-developed countries for national and commercial gain, with no return for the country providing the information? Can the poorer nations *prevent* information from leaving their countries until they can be certain it will not be used to their detriment?
>
> Will the new technology, *by its very nature,* manipulate us? Will governments and corporations be able to use it to manipulate us, or will we be able to manipulate the new technologies to serve the good of society? [p. 13].

What questions about computers and technology seem to be most relevant to continuing education and to educators of adults? We can list several, some of which have been alluded to earlier:

1. To what extent will people own home computers and use them, along with videotape, television, and telephone, as

home education centers? Given that this number may be considerable, how will such use affect the organization and operation of formal continuing education activities? What will this mean for the substantial number of people who will not be able to afford the new technology in their homes?

2. What will it mean to be an adult educator, with the prospect of large numbers of home computers? Will a major role be developing software for computers? Will a major effort be to counsel adult learners trying to make decisions about what to learn?

3. As television has influenced the learning styles of a generation of young adults—they tend to prefer visual material more often than older adults do (Ommen, Brainard, and Canfield, 1979)—will the adults of the next generation, who have experienced computers from their elementary school days on, prefer a learning style related to their computer experience?

4. As Weizenbaum and Wicklein warn, what responsibilities do we have as educators of adults to probe the deeper questions that humankind has always faced, questions of ethics and morals, questions that have social and political impact? Will a reliance on computer and other technology lead a population of learners and educators into believing that educational needs are being met, when the deeper, more difficult questions are overlooked?

Applied Perspective. Knowles (1980) represents a group of adult educators who have focused on an applied perspective of teaching and learning. Through his writings about "andragogy," Knowles has influenced thousands of adult education practitioners toward understanding practical applications of educating adults. Although one could criticize his approach of contrasting pedagogy (the education of children) with andragogy (the education of adults), he nevertheless caught the attention of adult educators in this country and in many others. He compares the assumptions of pedagogy and andragogy in the areas of concept of learner, role of learners' experience, readiness to learn, and orientation to learning (pp. 43-44). "Andragogy is premised on at least these four crucial assumptions about the characteristics of learners that are different from the assumptions on which traditional pedagogy is premised. These assumptions are that as individuals mature: (1) their self-concept moves from one of being a dependent personality toward being a self-directed human being; (2) they accumulate a growing reservoir of experience that becomes an increasingly rich resource for learning; (3) their readiness to learn becomes oriented increasingly to the developmental tasks of their social roles; and (4) their time perspective changes from one of postponed application of knowledge to immediacy of application, and accordingly, their orientation toward learning shifts from one of subject-centeredness to one of performance-centeredness" (pp. 44-45). Knowles has spent much of his career illustrating various types of practice that grow out of the assumptions he makes about adults as learners. His book *The Modern Practice of Adult Education* (1980) is a compendium of these practices.

Although many practitioners have followed and continue to follow Knowles's suggestions for conducting continuing education, questions can be raised. How useful is it to argue that adults and children are dramatically different in how they learn? (In recent years, Knowles, in his public statements, has conceded that there may be more similarities between child and adult learning than he first recognized). Is it correct to assume that all adults are striving to become self-directed learners? Or is it more likely that many adult learners, for one reason or another, prefer a certain dependency relationship or at least a co-working arrangement with an instructor? Is it possible that subject matter helps determine whether an adult wants to be a self-directed learner? Advanced mathematics or computer programming and skills such as swimming seem to be subject matter areas in which learners want instructor assistance.

Even though many questions can be raised about Knowles's andragogy, Cross (1981) says, "At the very least . . . [andragogy] identifies some characteristics of adult learners that deserve attention. It has been far more successful than most theory in gaining the attention of practitioners, and it has been moderately successful in sparking debate; it has not been especially successful, however, in stimulating research to test the assumptions" (pp. 227-228).

Integrated Perspective. Two researchers, Knox (1977) and Cross (1981), have drawn from a variety of disciplines to discuss teaching and learning in continuing education from an integrative perspective. Knox draws on research primarily from sociology, psychology, and physiology that relates to adult development and learning. He examined the research and discusses such concepts as stability and change, and development within the individual adult learner; ways in which the family and community contexts influence adult development and learning; adult life-cycle trends in performance in the family; how age trends relate to performance in education, occupation, and community; physical condition and health and the relation to sensory functioning and mental health; stability and change in personality characteristics, including self-concept and adjustment; how age relates to memory and problem solving; and how the various concepts from sociology, psychology, and physiology relate to one another.

Emphasis throughout Knox's work is on how continuing education practitioners can apply these research studies in their day-to-day work.

Cross's (1981) work, also drawing on several disciplines, focuses on the development of a conceptual framework for understanding adults as learners. Her framework "Characteristics of Adults as Learners" (CAL) includes two major components: personal characteristics and situational characteristics. Cross describes these two components this way: "The personal variables of CAL . . . are almost always considered continuous. They represent the gradual growth of children into adults and are expressed as growth or developmental continua along three dimensions: physical, psychological, and sociocultural" (p. 235). "Two characteristics sharply differentiate the learning *situation* of the adult from that of the child or adolescent; adults are typically part-time learners [in organized learning situations], and they are usually volunteers. Although the situational variables of CAL are not quite as discrete as they appear on the surface, they are usually expressed as dichotomies: part-time versus full-time learning and voluntary versus compulsory learning" (p. 235).

Cross suggests that educators need to consider different

educational strategies concerning each of the three categories
of personal characteristics. "The physiological continuum calls
for an educational stance that is largely adaptive and adjustive.
Physical aging, for instance, requires careful attention to trans-
portation and delivery systems, greater illumination, less audi-
tory confusion in the classroom" (p. 239). For the sociocultural
dimension Cross suggests that the educator's role is also adaptive and adjustive, as learners try to adjust to new adult life
phases. But for the developmental stage continuum Cross suggests a different strategy for the educator. "If one accepts a
hierarchy of developmental stages, and if one believes that the
role of educators is to help each individual develop to the highest possible level, then the role of educators is to challenge the
learner to move to increasingly advanced stages of personal development. This may mean creating the motivation for learning
through making the learner uncomfortable in her present assumptions" (p. 240). Thus the educator may at one time be
warm and accepting and at another time be challenging.

Institutions offering education for adults need to consider the part-time nature of most adult learners and their voluntary participation in most programs. Institutions need to consider when and where programs are offered to accommodate
part-time learners who have many other responsibilities in their
lives. They must also be conscious of what it means to participate as a volunteer learner as opposed to compulsory learning,
which is characteristic of youth education (and some continuing
education).

Comment. In this synoptic section I have examined some
of the literature of teaching and learning from a continuing education perspective. In doing synoptic analysis, it is important to
draw on a variety of sources for information. It is also important to reflect on what one has done and to raise questions, particularly about omissions. Some questions that could be raised,
after reflecting on the literature of teaching and learning in continuing education, are these:

1. To what extent is what is learned related to a person's
history and cultural setting? That is, do we learn some things
and not other things because of our past and the setting in

which we find ourselves? If we grew up on a farm in the Midwest during the 1930s, does this fact of history influence how we learn today? If we live today in a low-income section of Dallas, Texas, does this cultural fact influence how we learn? If the answer to these questions is yes, how do educators incorporate such information into their teaching?

2. To what extent is learning always a function of the explicit or implicit purposes of continuing education that are predominant at a particular time? In other words, to what extent is learning related to and in service of the predominant purposes for continuing education outlined in the previous chapter?

3. To what extent should the learner have control of the learning situation, rather than the control always being in the hands of the educator and/or the educational institution?

4. Will new technology, such as computers, have such a dramatic effect on education that we must rethink what teaching means, who educators are, and how the learning process takes place?

Normative Analysis

By doing a critical analysis of our teaching approaches and our understanding of adult learning, we can gain insight into our practice. After such an analysis, we often raise critical questions about what we do, and we begin looking for alternative ways of teaching. A synoptic analysis provides a source of alternative responses. In the examples given, I have illustrated how one might analyze two prominent approaches to teaching/learning in continuing education—the humanistic approach and the behavioristic approach. Following this critical analysis, I showed, by example, how one might draw widely on literature to obtain a broad perspective and a variety of alternatives about teaching and learning in continuing education.

In this normative analysis section I illustrate, by means of example, how one might develop a position about teaching and learning in continuing education built around the work of the philosopher Jurgen Habermas. I must underline that this is but one way of doing a normative analysis. Each practitioner in continuing education is challenged to reflect on the results of his or her critical and synoptic analyses and to develop a normative position that fits and can be defended. Recall from Chapter Two that normative analysis is concerned with asking "what should be" questions. The central question here is, what approach should I take in teaching adults?

Let us explore, then, one approach to developing a normative position about teaching and learning in continuing education. The German philosopher Jurgen Habermas (1972) presents a way of looking at teaching and learning that helps us see what is missing in the present way we discuss and practice education of adults. Habermas presents three "categories of processes of inquiry"—his words for approaches to teaching and learning: (1) technical, (2) practical, and (3) emancipatory. Adult educator Jack Mezirow (1981), an interpreter of Habermas, writes, "Habermas suggests that differences in the very nature of these three interests mandate fundamentally different methodologies of systematic objective inquiry. By extension, each learning domain suggests to me a different mode of personal learning and different learning needs. These imply three different functions for adult education concerned with facilitating such learning" (p. 4).

The first category of learning relates to how one controls and manipulates one's environment. Much of the discussion of learning presented earlier in this chapter and the majority of the purposes presented for continuing education in the previous chapter fit within this category of learning. Technical learning often relates to a job or career; it helps one perform various tasks; it is often related to specific, identifiable outcomes. For instance, if one strives to become a computer programmer, there are various skills to be learned and much information to obtain before one can perform in this role.

Habermas's second category of learning, which he calls "practical," might better be identified as interactive or communicative. Here the emphasis is not on technical control—being able to perform some particular task, for example. Rather, the emphasis is on obtaining meaning from communication. "Here the meaning of the validity of propositions is not constituted in the frame of reference of technical control . . . access to the facts is provided by the understanding of meaning, not observation" (Habermas, 1972, p. 309). Habermas suggests one does this by applying historical-hermeneutic approaches. Hermeneutics, a branch of theology, is concerned with deriving meaning from textual analysis. As Mezirow (1981) suggests, "The historical-hermeneutic disciplines differ from the empirical-analytic sciences in the 'content' studied, methods of inquiry, and criteria for assessing alternative interpretations. They include descriptive social science, history, esthetics, legal, ethnographic, literary, and other studies interpreting the meaning of communicative experience" (p. 5). That learning which involves the examination of literature, as in Great Books discussions, would seem to fall in this category, as would much of liberal arts education for adults, particularly when the emphasis is on group discussion, interaction, and deriving meaning from the material studied as well as from interactions.

It is the third category, emancipatory learning, where I believe the field of continuing education does little. Emancipatory learning is that which frees people from personal, institutional, or environmental forces that prevent them from seeing new directions, from gaining control of their lives, their society, and their world.

Emancipatory Learning. Emancipatory learning has a critical, an integrative, and an action perspective. The critical perspective of emancipatory learning involves questioning present situations, examining assumptions, challenging current ways of viewing the world, and analyzing knowledge and our present ways of knowing. As philosopher José Ortega y Gasset (1960) wrote, "To know is to be not content with things as presented to us but to seek beyond their appearance for their being. This 'being' of things is a strange condition: it is not made clear in things, but on the contrary, it throbs hidden within them, beneath them, beyond them . . . [knowing] is a refusal to be content with what can be seen, a denying that what can be seen is enough, a demand for the invisible, the 'beyond' " (pp. 67–68).

Another way of describing the critical perspective of emancipatory learning is to say that emancipatory learning involves increasing one's awareness. As the English philosopher R. W. K. Paterson (1979) suggests, "To foster the development of the adult as a person, then, to educate him, is to extend the scope and enrich the quality of his awareness, and when we deem an activity to be educational in character, we do so by virtue of its pursuit and achievement of this governing principle" (p. 67). Paterson says that any educational activity that does not involve development of awareness cannot properly be called adult education.

Freire's (1970) ideas about consciousness raising can be, in some ways, related to Paterson's development of awareness. But Freire places considerable emphasis on the social and political context in which education occurs. For Freire, an educational program includes a consciousness-raising phase that he calls "thematic investigation." Examples of themes might be work, poverty, and world peace.

Emancipatory learning also means drawing widely from a variety of disciplines, from one's experience, and from one's own feelings—the integrative perspective. As the philosopher J. Krishnamurti (1953) reminded us, "We may be highly educated, but if we are without deep integration of thought and feeling, our lives are incomplete, contradictory, and torn with many fears; and as long as education does not cultivate an integrated outlook on life, it has very little significance" (p. 11).

Emancipatory learning integrates a variety of points of view; it brings together opposing positions, it examines the past and the present, it includes knowledge from a wide sweep of disciplines, and, very importantly, it includes one's own views and feelings. Ortega y Gasset (1960) reminded us, "We need a complete perspective, with foreground and background, not a maimed and partial landscape, not a horizon from which the lure of the great distances has been cut away. Lacking a set of cardinal points, our footsteps lack direction" (p. 66).

Emancipatory learning also includes an action dimension. One does not just read and study and reflect; one acts on what one is coming to know. Thus, to practice emancipatory learning, one must do more than accumulate information—one must act on that information. And it is only through the action that one really comes to know something. Depending on what one is concerned about, emancipatory learning may involve actions designed to change certain structures in society, such as modifying institutions. Action may also involve changing social situations in which people live. The action perspective of emancipatory learning is based on several assumptions: that human beings are free to act on their world; that human beings, differing from other living creatures, have the alternative of being able to create and modify their world; that they have the ability to reflect on their past, to be conscious of the present, and to make plans for the future; and that as persons work toward changing social structures and social situations, they themselves change. These personal changes involve, most profoundly, movement from passive, isolated persons to active subjects capable of learning and acting together.

Why is little attention given to emancipatory learning, which is concerned with thought and examination, with analysis and questioning, and with action, rather than solely with acceptance of what educators present? At least three reasons can be offered: influence of the dominant paradigm of today's society, influence of previous formal schooling, and selective inattention.

In the previous chapter I discussed characteristics of the dominant paradigm in our society—the assumptions that guide people, often without their being aware of it. I listed such assumptions as the importance of specialization, the reverence for efficiency, reliance on the scientific method as the only valid approach to knowledge, accumulation of material goods as a symbol of personal success, and preparation for career as the purpose of education. These assumptions guide not only the selection of aims for continuing education but also how educators view the teaching/learning process.

The dominant paradigm of our society favors the first and second of Habermas's three approaches to teaching and learning—the technical and "practical" approaches. The dominant paradigm tends to discourage, or at least influences the educator and learner to ignore, the third approach—emancipatory education. Why? Emancipatory learning, by its nature, challenges the status quo. Emancipatory learning helps learners identify the prevailing assumptions of our society and then question them critically, offer alternatives to them, and act on them. Emancipatory learning is often critical of educational institutions and educators. Emancipatory learning may be critical of educational policy makers and other supporters of educational activity. The practice of emancipatory learning is usually uncomfortable for educators and the institutions they represent. It is also uncomfortable for noneducational institutions in society, for emancipatory learning often challenges them, too. The extent that educators and educational institutions are influenced by the present dominant assumptions of our society is the extent that emancipatory learning will not occur.

Previous formal schooling usually has a negative influence on an adult's practice of emancipatory learning. Richer (1981-82) believes that four categories of assumptions, which public schools follow, negatively influence emancipatory learning: authoritarianism, fragmentation of physical and social reality, ethic of interindividual competition, and reinforcement of traditional sex differences.

Within the area of authoritarianism, he says the following assumptions prevail:

- The teacher initiates most classroom interaction.
- There is a heavy discipline aspect to all interaction.
- Punishment is a social control device.
- Transmission, evaluation, and control are all in the hands of the teacher.

Within physical and social reality one finds the following assumptions:

- Knowledge is viewed as external to the learner.
- Knowledge from within the school is legitimate, knowledge from outside the school is not.

The ethic of interindividual competition includes such manifestations as—

- Awarding of grades, stars, and other symbols of individual achievement.
- Competitive games played.

Sex differences are manifested in—

- Teachers' tendencies to reinforce "masculine" behavior in males, "feminine" behavior in females.
- Tendency toward male superiority in many textbooks (pp. 46-47).

Greene (1973) believes that the school setting is often one in which, for a variety of reasons, teachers find themselves simply surviving. "They concentrate on the daily routines, trying to be cool and disengaged, as functional and impersonal as machines. . . . Most commonly, they behave like clerks, subjects of a remote authority that issues orders, supervises, and asks little more than conformity to custom, to the prevailing 'law.' They are powerless and they accede" (pp. 4-5). How is it possible for a young person to experience emancipatory learning in a situation such as Greene describes?

Apple (1979) believes two conditions in the schools adversely influence attempts at emancipatory learning: a belief that conflict is taboo and a belief that children should be the recipients of values and what institutions have to offer, not creators and re-creators of values and institutions (p. 86). In many schools "a basic assumption seems to be that conflict among groups of people is *inherently* and fundamentally bad and we should strive to eliminate it *within* the established framework of institutions, rather than seeing conflict and contradiction as the basic 'driving forces' in society" (p. 87). As an example Apple cites the way science is taught in many schools. He says science is taught as a domain of knowledge and a group of techniques. "Like all communities, [science] is governed by norms, values, and principles that are both overtly seen and covertly felt. By being made up of individuals and groups of scholars, it also has had a significant history of both intellectual and interpersonal struggle. Often the conflict is generated by the introduction of a new and usually quite revolutionary paradigm that challenges the basic meaning structures that were previously accepted by the particular body of scientists, often, thereby, effectively dividing the scholarly community" (p. 88). Thus, by the time these children become adults, they have come to see education as a collection of information and procedures that are viewed as givens. The idea that all this may be questioned is remote to the adult who has been formally educated to think otherwise.

Still another reason that many adults do not practice emancipatory learning is what Harry Stack Sullivan (1956) called "selective inattention." Sullivan posed the question: How is it possible for people to go through life facing so many opportunities to learn and yet learn so little from these experiences (p. 38)? According to Sullivan, people are practicing selective inattention, "which to a great extent enables us to stay as we are, despite remarkable experiences that befall us, simply by keeping the attention on something else—in other words, by *controlling awareness* of the events that impinge upon us" (p. 38).

I agree with Sullivan that many opportunities to practice emancipatory learning, even to be aware that there is such a thing, are not perceived by many adults. Why does selective inattention occur? First, human beings simply cannot always be aware of everything that goes on around them. There is no possible way to do that, and it is not necessary. What is necessary is the ability to sort out the irrelevant from the relevant. Here is where the discussion of society's dominant paradigm and the influence of one's previous schooling applies. As we are guided by society's dominant assumptions—and we all are to a greater or lesser extent—we will perceive certain things and not others. We have all been in situations in which, when we look back at them, we say, "How could I have overlooked that?" We overlooked it because the event fell outside the assumptions of our society and outside what our schooling and other life experiences had taught us to expect.

Society's dominant paradigm and one's previous schooling influence emancipatory learning in at least two ways. First, they influence one's ability to accept the idea that there can be such a thing as emancipatory learning. Second, they influence what is perceived that may contribute to one's emancipatory learning. This leads us to discuss the process of emancipatory learning: How does it occur, and what role is there for the educator in assisting the process?

Process of Emancipatory Learning. Someone who participates in emancipatory learning is moving from something to something else. To say it another way, one is becoming liberated from something, an idea, a way of thinking, a set of assumptions, an approach to practice, and replacing this something with a different idea, a different way of thinking, and so on.

The process includes these phases: becoming aware, exploring alternatives, transition, and integration. *Becoming aware* means realizing that something is wrong, that there is a certain discomfort in one's life, that things could be better, that a societal situation could be different, that certain policies are not working properly. The process of becoming aware is Freire's consciousness raising, mentioned above. Becoming aware is what Ferguson (1980) describes as anything that "shakes up the old understanding of the world, the old priorities" (p. 89). Roger von Oech, a creativity specialist, says, "We all need an occasional whack on the side of the head to shake us out of routine patterns, to force us to rethink our problems, and to stimulate us to ask new questions that may lead to other answers" (1983, p. 12). Von Oech suggests several examples of events that may help one become aware: traveling to another country, failing to receive a merit raise, asking questions that are the reverse of those ordinarily asked, putting together two ideas that everyone says should not be put together (pp. 13–15).

Becoming aware means making the ordinary extraordinary, making the common uncommon. It may mean becoming aware of contradictions in one's life, in one's community, in one's government. For example, it may mean becoming aware of a governmental policy that advocates literacy education for all adults needing it but then cuts budgets in this area, assuming that for-profit institutions can provide a larger amount of literacy education. The policy fails to mention that many people with low literacy also have low incomes and cannot afford the fees required for their education.

Techniques an educator can follow to encourage this awareness phase of emancipatory learning include having learners work in small groups where ideas are presented on given topics and then are challenged by participants. Rather than an accepting attitude in the small group where someone presents information for others to dutifully write down, all ideas and information presented are challenged and discussed. Such close questioning by an educator and other learners can often help everyone in the group become aware of ideas, beliefs, and assumptions that he or she had not thought of before. Another technique is to have the educator assume a position of questioner and challenger as well as presenter of ideas in the group. For this approach to be successful, the educator must create a learning environment in which he or she is not viewed as having all the answers. The environment must be one in which all are learners and all are teachers, with the roles constantly shifting. Still another technique is to provide a variety of teaching approaches, ranging from the small-group seminars to having people go into the community to videotape evidence of particular community problems, which is brought back for discussion.

Exploring alternatives is accomplished by searching for new ways of doing things, new answers, new concepts, new ways of organizing one's world views. This can be an extremely trying phase, for one is at the same time bringing into question old ways of thinking and searching for new approaches. "Warily or enthusiastically, having sensed that there is something worth finding, the individual sets out to look for it. The first serious step, however small, is empowering and significant" (Ferguson, 1980, p. 92).

Exploring alternatives, like the other phases in the process of emancipatory learning, can be an individual activity or a group activity. That is, a person can explore alternatives that apply only to him or her or, working in a group on a community problem, can explore alternatives for group action.

The educator can assist during this phase of the process by providing an awareness of alternatives for an individual or a group to consider. By asking questions, the educator can help the learners explore various alternatives so they come to know them in some depth. It is important during this phase of the process that the educator not become an advocate of a particular alternative. The individual or the group should look at alternatives without having to consider one alternative more important than another just because an educator has advocated it.

It is usually during this phase of emancipatory learning that the clear decision is made that the old will be left behind for one or more of the new alternatives. This leads into phase three of the process, transition.

Transition is likely the most difficult phase, for it is then that the old is left behind and a new approach, a new way of thinking, a new alternative is adopted. "Like the troubled society struggling to remake itself with old tools and structures, the individual tries at first to improve the situation rather than change it, to reform rather than transform" (Ferguson, 1980, p. 93). Deciding that the old must be left behind, an idea or an assumption that may have served one for many years, is a wrenching experience. The first attempt is to not leave behind the old idea, but to modify it, change it in some way so that it can be kept. As Marris (1974) points out, "Whether the crisis of disorientation affects only an individual, or a group, or society as a whole, it has a fundamentally similar dynamic. It provokes a conflict between contradictory impulses—to return to the past and to forget it altogether. Each, in itself, would be ultimately self-destructive, either by denying the reality of present circumstances or by denying the experience on which the sense of self rests. But their interaction forces the bereaved to search to and fro, until they are reconciled by reformulating and reintegrating past attachments" (pp. 151–152).

The process of leaving behind and accepting something new is a process of unlearning, and it tends to go counter to what most of us have been taught. We view development as gain, not loss. And to unlearn, we lose, we leave something behind. Our Western way of thinking applauds building on previous structures, building on familiar ideas, rather than leaving behind structures and ideas and shifting to new ones. This is not to say that building on previous structures and previous ideas is inappropriate, for many times it is most appropriate to do so. For instance, learning how to use a new piece of equipment in one's job, such as a microcomputer, may be trying at the time. But one is building on previous experiences and incorporating this new device into already well-established ways of accomplishing certain tasks. (As I argued earlier, computers and their applications may indeed influence radical new ways of thinking and doing and thus may cause one to reexamine present structures and ways of thinking once a person has bought a computer.)

The transition phase (when something is clearly left behind) is a difficult one because a person or a group that is going through it has in some ways lost one of its compasses, a guiding set of assumptions, perhaps. These assumptions may have served as a foundation for action and for viewing the future, and without this foundation there is loss and confusion. "The reality that is left behind . . . is not just a picture on the wall. It is a sense of which way is up and which way is down; it is a sense of which way is forward and which way is backward. It is, in short, a way of orienting oneself and of moving forward into the future. . . . The old sense of life as 'going somewhere' breaks down, and we feel like shipwrecked sailors on some existential atoll" (Bridges, 1980, p. 102).

One can equate what happens during the transition phase of emancipatory learning to the grieving process on losing a loved one. Meyers (1984) has studied the processes by which small groups leave behind old patterns and move to new ones. A similar process can be applied to individuals who are in the transition phase. Meyers writes, "Experiences of grief are evoked when the group's ability to continue the established pattern of meaning is threatened; discontinuity is becoming more apparent than continuity. Grieving results from the exchange being made between the group's prior and predictable self-concept and its not-yet, unpredictable future self-concept. Grieving results from the classic conflict between conservation and innovation" (p. 1).

Bridges (1980) calls the time between deciding to leave something behind and fully accepting an alternative position a "neutral zone." "One of the difficulties of being in transition in the modern world is that we have lost our appreciation for this gap in the continuity of existence. . . . We need not feel defensive about this apparently unproductive time-out at turning points in our lives, for the neutral zone is meant to be a moratorium from the conventional activity of our everyday existence. . . . In the apparently aimless activity of our time alone, we are doing important inner business" (pp. 112-114).

This transition time (neutral zone) is extremely important in the process of emancipatory learning. It is relatively easy for a person or a group to slide back toward its old assumptions and its old ways of thinking when faced with the often terrible uncertainty of something new. It is also difficult for a person or a group to recognize that the feeling of loss for old ideas and old ways of thinking is a natural state of affairs and that time will heal. "The more radical the changes which evolve, the more important [it is for us to] recognize the element of bereavement . . . in the process of a major reconstruction" (Marris, 1974, p. 151).

Educators can assist individuals and groups who are in the transition phase of emancipatory learning in several ways. One of the most important is for the educator to recognize that the transition phase takes time and that the learner experiences a sense of loss similar to bereavement. Thus an important role for the educator is one of patience and support. The educator can help those in transition understand that what they are feeling is normal and that others before them have experienced the same thing. But the educator cannot speed up the process, nor can the educator help resolve the reintegration on behalf of the learner or the group. Marris (1974) writes about three principles for management of change that should guide the educator: "First, the process of reform must always expect and even encourage conflict. Whenever people are confronted with change, they need the opportunity to react, to articulate their ambivalent feelings and work out their own sense of it. Second, the process must respect the autonomy of different kinds of experience, so that groups of people can organize without the intrusion of alien conceptions. Third, there must be time and patience, because the conflicts involve not only the accommodation of diverse interests but the realization of an essential continuity in the structure of meaning. Each of these principles corresponds with an aspect of grief, as a crisis of reintegration which can neither be escaped, nor resolved by anyone on behalf of another, nor hurried" (p. 156).

Integration, the fourth phase of emancipatory learning, involves becoming comfortable with and acting on the new ideas, new assumptions, new ways of thinking that have emerged from the transition phase. "It is when the endings and the time of fallow neutrality are finished that we can launch ourselves out anew, changed and renewed by the destruction of the old life-phase and the journey through the nowhere" (Bridges, 1980, p. 134). Sometimes it is difficult to know when integration has occurred; other times, a flash of insight strikes us and we know the new ideas we have are the right ones for us. Often we know that integration has taken place when we are more comfortable with our work, when we feel less stressed, when we feel that what we are now doing has more meaning for us and for others.

The entire process of emancipatory learning is in many ways similar to scientific revolutions and paradigm shifting as Kuhn (1970) has analyzed them. "Both kinds of revolution [changes in science and emancipatory learning] arise from the internal decay of the preceding construction of reality; both are characteristically, if not necessarily, first formulated long before the established order has exhausted its attempts to rationalize the anomalies and contradictions within its own framework; and both are ultimately accepted when these rationalizations seem to lead to a dead end" (Marris, 1974, p. 163).

Summary

Following the model introduced earlier, I have shown how one might critically analyze statements about teaching and learning in continuing education. Using the principles of synoptic analysis, I illustrated how one might describe principles and approaches to teaching and learning from such perspectives as psychology, sociology, anthropology, and biology. Then, in the normative analysis section, I demonstrated how one might take a particular approach to teaching and learning and develop a "should be" perspective. Other approaches may certainly be advocated, but I chose to argue for emancipatory learning. Then I illustrated what it is, why it is important, what phases are involved, and the contributions that educators might make to the process.

Teaching/learning is the soul of continuing education. Too often we as practitioners in continuing education are content to accept whatever the vogue approach to teaching might happen to be and go on our merry ways. As educators, we have the responsibility to understand what we do and why we do it. The processes discussed and illustrated in this chapter are provided as a starting place for the educator interested in becoming more self-directed.

8

Analyzing
Program Development
Processes

$\approx\approx\approx\approx\approx\approx\approx\approx\approx\approx\approx\approx\approx$

Two questions have faced continuing education programmers for years: What should be the content of educational programs, and how should educational programs be planned? In this chapter I will examine both questions. I will follow suggestions for critical, synoptic, and normative analysis, as was done in the previous three chapters. But this time I will not try to do the analysis in discrete, linear activities. That is, one can (1) examine a statement critically (critical analysis), (2) search for information about the statement from several sources (synoptic analysis), and (3) then make normative judgments about it (normative analysis). In reality, when we do an analysis of a statement or a situation in continuing education, we often apply all three approaches—critical, synoptic, and normative—simultaneously. This is the approach I will follow in this chapter. I will introduce several statements about content and about programming approaches for continuing education and then analyze them.

A Sampling of Content Statements

1. *Continuing education is transferring information from a source or depository (an educator, book, or videotape, for example) to a learner.*

To some educators of adults, education is little more than moving information from one place to another. In fact, the phrase often used to describe various forms of education, such as an educational telephone network or a series of courses taught off campus, is *delivery system*. What are the assumptions inherent in the metaphor "delivery system," the moving of information from one place to another? (1) Information can be moved intact from a depository to a learner. (2) Knowledge is something that is outside the learner.

Let us first examine the difference between information and knowledge. If we believe that the process of learning includes attempting to derive one's own meaning from information and applying it, then that which is communicated remains information to the learner until the learner does something with the information. Suppose, for example, that I am conducting a program on acid rain, its causes, and its possible solutions. I have arranged a panel of experts to explore this question from several perspectives: a representative from the electric power industry, a water chemist, an environmentalist, and an economist. Each of these persons presents his or her knowledge about acid rain. But though the panelists are presenting knowledge from their own viewpoints, from the viewpoint of the people in the audience, the learners, these experts are presenting information. Until the participants in the program begin to think about what is said, to relate the information to their own situations—increases in electric bills, perhaps the possibility of more nuclear power plants to replace coal-fired plants that contribute to acid rain— the information does not become knowledge. In addition, because we all have different histories, different world views, different social and cultural influences, the knowledge that we develop from the information we receive will sometimes differ from the knowledge held by the experts. Hence we educators are sometimes surprised, and even concerned at times, that those who participate in educational programs do not seem to be gaining the same knowledge that we provided. In fact, if we follow tightly defined evaluation systems, in which we attempt to relate input to output, we may be chagrined because what we taught is not what has been received.

We can also examine the phrase *delivery system* as a

metaphor. The postal system is a delivery system; it collects mail and delivers it (most of the time) to people to whom it is addressed. Commercial television is a delivery system, producing programs and making them widely available. The trucking industry collects and distributes goods throughout the country and is thus a delivery system. But is information a commodity to be packaged, collected, and distributed widely, through a variety of methods and means? Many would argue that it is—we pay money for information, do we not, as we do for other goods? But let us make a distinction between delivering information and delivering education. As I argued earlier, the information that we deliver as educators remains as information to the recipient until the person acts on this information in some way. By acting on the information—thinking about it, relating it to previous information, and perhaps trying to apply it—it becomes knowledge for the recipient. Because we have developed an educational system in this country that has placed so much importance on information that comes from experts, many people have tried to apply this information directly, without trying to make sense out of it, without trying to derive their own meaning from it. Thus we as educators have sometimes been trapped into believing that the relatively simple task of delivering information is the sum total of an educational activity. As I pointed out in the previous chapter, education must be more than providing information.

With the advent of increasing amounts of educational technology, particularly the microcomputer, it is becoming easier to store and deliver vast amounts of information. Thus our task as educators, if we agree education is more than delivering information, becomes more difficult. There is also the danger, as we rely increasingly on technology to assist us in our educational activities, to consider only that information which can be electronically packaged. Can we expect that educational technology such as the microcomputer will assist educators and learners in probing questions of ethics and morals, questions of social consequence and political direction? (See the previous chapter for discussion of these issues.)

The second assumption of educational programming as a

delivery system is that information is outside the learner. It should be evident from the foregoing discussion that much of what we know comes from within us; its sources are our history, our experiences, and our social setting. Often an educational activity need not introduce outside information but, rather, may concentrate on questions and activities to help the learner become aware of what he or she already knows or to find new meaning in information that the learner already possesses.

2. *Society is experiencing an information explosion, making the task of continuing education increasingly more difficult.*

It is obviously true that the amount of information available is growing at ever-increasing rates. The metaphor *information explosion* is an interesting one. *Explosion* is usually associated with something harmful, and it also usually refers to a breaking apart, a larger piece splitting into many smaller pieces. Quite the opposite meaning is usually associated with *information explosion*; we generally view it as a good thing, a sign of progress in society, and an accumulation of information, not a breaking apart of present information.

Unfortunately, educators often believe that because the supply of information is increasing so rapidly, this vast supply must be transmitted to learners. The educator accepts this growing supply of information without asking such fundamental questions as: Which information is worthy of inclusion in a particular educational program, which is accurate, and which is important? These questions are not easy to answer, and yet the concerned and responsible educator must wrestle with them and formulate answers. An important role an educator can play is to help learners wade through the flood of information these learners encounter and assist them in developing criteria about which information to accept and which to reject. These criteria can include such factors as relevance, usefulness, cost of application, ease of application, and accuracy of the information.

3. *The only information worthy of including in an educational program is that which can be traced to an expert or to scientific research.*

This belief has its source in a view of scientism that sees information as "a rigorous interchange of reason and systematically acquired experience" (Goldberg, 1983, p. 17). This rather narrow view of the source of information developed as a hybrid of empiricism and rationalism. "Empiricism holds, essentially, that the experience of the senses is the only reliable basis for knowing; rationalism contends that reasoning is the prime avenue to truth. . . . Since experience can be deceptive, information is scrutinized with rigorous logic; since reason is not entirely flawless, tentative conclusions—hypotheses—are put to the empirical test with controlled experiments subject to repeated verification. For this . . . to work, the data should be quantifiable and the players should be objective, thus keeping biases, emotions, and opinions from contaminating the findings" (Goldberg, 1983, p. 17).

Goldberg argues that the scientistic view of information is too narrow and that along with science we must also include information rooted in intuition. He maintains that intuition as an information source is also integral to science. But because so many people believe that worthy information comes only from science, Goldberg says much valuable and worthwhile information is overlooked. "If your only cognitive tools are rational-empirical, your vision will be restricted to what can be analyzed and measured. Ask the grand metaphysical questions about human identity and the nature of reality, and materialistic answers will come back. The self comes to be seen as a catalogue of analyzable personality traits, and the cosmos becomes a collection of objects separated from the self, an incomplete vision with consequences that range from shortchanging human potential to pillaging nature" (p. 25).

From the perspective of persons developing knowledge—that is, making sense out of information in a personal way—Goldberg compares the rational approach and the intuitive approach. "Rational thought is drawn out over time; it takes place in a definable sequence of steps with a beginning, middle, and end. It is linear. It requires effort and deliberate intention. By contrast, intuition is experienced as nonsequential. It is a single event as opposed to a series, a snapshot as opposed to a motion picture. And it just seems to happen, often when least expected, without the application of specific rules. When you arrive at a conclusion through rational thought, you can usually trace the mental process backward and identify the antecedent steps. Intuition is inexplicable. The intuiter might be able to provide a plausible explanation for what led to his knowledge, but he would be reasoning retroactively and couldn't be sure that the explanation matched the actual process" (p. 32).

Ornstein (1976) compares the development of rational knowledge and intuitive knowledge this way: "The logical mode of knowledge operates sequentially, arriving at truth inferentially, proceeding logically from one element to another. Intuition operates simultaneously, is concerned with the sets of relations among elements, which receive their meaning from the overall holistic context. Reason, then, primarily involves an analysis of discrete elements, inferentially (sequentially) linked; intuition involves a simultaneous perception of the whole. . . . It is not the individual, discrete objects, elements, or even ideas which are themselves changed in the shift from a logical mode of consciousness to an intuitive one. Rather, it is the relationship between the elements which change, and the interpretation of a given bit of sensory data may be different depending upon the context" (pp. 46–47).

In addition to broadening an understanding of how knowledge is developed, research on quantum mechanics, or the new physics, has challenged the old definitions of scientific knowledge. "The 'new physics' . . . began with Max Planck's theory of quanta in 1900, and relativity, which began with Albert Einstein's special theory of relativity in 1905" (Zukav, 1979, p. 25). The new physics raises several questions about the nature of knowledge, building on the work of Newton's "old physics" but also challenging this old view of science. Pure objectivity was one assumption of the old physics. But as Zukav points out, "The concept of scientific objectivity rests upon the assumption of an external world which is 'out there' as opposed to an 'I' which is 'in here.' (This way of perceiving, which puts other people 'out there,' makes it very lonely 'in here.') According to this view, Nature, in all her diversity is 'out there.' The task of the scientist is to observe the 'out there' as objectively as possible. To observe something objectively means to see it as it would appear to an observer who has no prejudices about what he observes [but] according to quantum mechanics there is no such thing as objectivity. We cannot eliminate ourselves from the picture. We are a part of nature, and when we study nature there is no way around the fact that nature is studying itself" (pp. 55–56).

Capra (1975) says, "In modern physics, the universe is . . . experienced as a dynamic, inseparable whole which always includes the observer in an essential way. In this experience, the traditional concepts of space and time, of isolated objects, and of cause and effect lose their meaning'" (p. 70). In terms of interrelationships, Capra writes, "Modern physics shows us . . . that material objects are not distinct entities, but are inseparably linked to their environment; that their properties can only be understood in terms of their interaction with the rest of the world" (p. 195).

In summary, what can we say about content for continuing education: What guidelines can we relate to assist the continuing education programmer?

Knowledge is an extremely broad concept. There is a close relationship between learner and knowledge. What is knowledge to an educator may be only information to the learner, until the learner is able to give meaning to the information. Knowledge can also have a process dimension; one can learn to criticize one's knowledge. In fact, the process of converting information to knowledge often entails making judgments about the value and worth of particular information.

The new physics suggests that knowledge cannot be purely objective, that all knowledge is related to and is influenced by other knowledge. Sources of knowledge include the researcher and the educator as well as the learner who attempts to make meaning out of experience. Knowledge may have empirical/rational roots, intuitive roots, or some combination of these.

Concerning content and the preceding discussion, what guidelines can we offer the programmer? (1) Be open to a wide range of content from a multitude of sources. Do not be influenced to include only that content which is available from experts in a given field, but do not exclude content from these experts, either. Recognize the importance of content that learners already have and make a provision in programming strategies so that learner-held content can be shared. (2) Realize that an educational program is more than delivering information to learners. Opportunities must be provided for learners to question, challenge, and make meaning of information—so that information can become knowledge for them.

Statements from Program Planning

1. *Continuing education programs should be based on needs.*

This statement is used often as a slogan by continuing education practitioners. Because the statement is general and is so often used, much confusion surrounds it. Several questions can be raised about the statement: What is the definition of need? Whose needs? What approaches are used in defining needs?

Needs are defined in a variety of ways. Maslow (1970) defined a hierarchy of needs including survival, security, social, self-esteem, and self-actualization needs. Monette (1977) identified four categories of needs: basic human needs, felt and expressed needs, normative needs, and comparative needs. Basic human needs can be described as drives or as tensions that humans have for which they seek gratification—for instance, the needs for food and shelter. Felt and expressed needs can be described as wants or desires and are sometimes referred to as interests. When someone says she wants to learn how to swim, she is expressing a felt need. "A need may be called normative when it constitutes a deficiency or gap between a 'desirable' standard and the standard that actually exists. The individual or group that falls short of the desirable standard is said to be in need" (Monette, 1977, p. 118). Comparative needs are those that result when one compares services a particular group receives with those another group receives. If two groups have similar characteristics and one receives certain services and the other does not, the second group is said to be in need.

Another way of examining the meaning of the term need

is to ask, Whose needs? In the literature of continuing education, needs are applied to individuals, to organizations and institutions, to communities, and to the larger society. When applied to individuals, the term is usually used in two ways: (1) interchangeably with *want, desire,* or *interest* or (2) to indicate a gap between a present situation (gap in knowledge, attitude, or skill) compared with some ideal state.

Organizational and institutional needs may include communication problems among staff members, plans for future development (growth, decline, new directions), and lack of future goals (Hall, 1980, pp. 207–212). Community and societal needs reflect such problems as inadequate medical facilities, unemployment, insufficient housing, lack of land-use plans, and ground water pollution.

A variety of approaches for identifying needs (usually called "needs assessment") are included in the literature of continuing education. Nowlen (1980) lists four approaches to needs assessment: (1) Offer a sample program and then record how many and what types of adults enroll. (2) Conduct an interest inventory. For instance, near the end of a program, ask participants to fill out a form indicating which topics or programs they would be interested in attending in the future. (3) Ask experts who are knowledgeable about a particular category of adults to estimate their educational needs. For instance, social workers may be able to report on educational needs of low-income people with whom they work. (4) In the employment setting, needs can be assessed during the performance review process. An employee and his or her supervisor compare actual performance with desired performance and make decisions about educational needs required for improving performance (Nowlen, 1980, pp. 31–32).

Grabowski (1982) identifies six models for needs assessment: "(a) Self-fulfillment—these models appeal to individuals' interests and desires on a random and selective basis. (b) Individual appraisals—individuals, on their own or in collaboration with others, determine their own learning needs. (c) System discrepancy—deficiencies or gaps are identified between the current condition and the desired state of individuals. (d) Diagnosis

—unmet as well as met needs are examined to determine which deficiencies would be corrected. (e) Analysis—a direction of improvement is determined based on the given situation of individuals. (f) Democratic—groups of individuals specify needs through a group process such as consensus or voting" (p. 62). Grabowski goes on to outline a series of methods that can be followed to gather data about needs. But, he cautions, "It is recommended that, whichever techniques are employed, they be verified for validity and reliability" (p. 63).

Robinson (1979, p. 65) lists nine methods for assessing needs, ranging from individual assessment—"The process involves learners in building their own competency models for self-development and then comparing their present situations against the models"—to professional literature—"Often professional journals or articles raise questions or produce new insights that lead directly to an increased awareness of learning needs. A review of professional literature can help identify needs in special fields or activities." Also included are analysis and performance review—"A job analysis provides specific and precise information about jobs and performance" (p. 66).

It is clear from the continuing education literature that educators of adults believe it is important to do a needs assessment as a part of the program-planning process and that procedures are available for carrying out the process. But several questions can be raised. Is the process of needs assessment as straightforward and value-free as the various procedures suggest? Indeed, is it possible to determine needs, particularly those that are defined as real needs, following straightforward empirical procedures? Recall that real needs are defined as those representing a gap between some present situation and a desired or ideal situation. One may, following empirical procedures of various types, assess the present situation of learners—how many have incomes below the poverty level, how many are unemployed, and so forth. But to determine the desired or ideal part of the need equation is not an empirical matter. Determining the desired or ideal situation concerning learners is a normative process. And as Deardon (1971) writes, norms "can neither be 'discovered' nor empirically refuted, since they indicate how things ought to be in various ways. Questions as to desirable standards, proper functioning, desirable rules, or what appropriateness and efficiency are cannot be determined by observation or experiment, though this does not mean they are arbitrary or insusceptible of being reasoned about. It does mean, however, that conflicts of opinion may be expected here, that in some cases the conflict may be very intractable and that . . . decisions may be involved, not just discoveries" (p. 94).

Thus it is not a simple task to discover what the ideal or desired portion of the need equation ought to be. A related question must also be raised. If the so-called real needs for learners cannot be determined following the standard need-assessment approaches as outlined above, how *can* they be determined, and who should be involved in the determination? One answer is that the educator has the responsibility for determining the desired component of need assessment. In some instances this is surely appropriate, for the educator may be well aware of the research in a particular area, may have experience with the content and its application, and may be the proper person to decide on the norms. For example, if an instructor is teaching a group of ambulance attendants procedures for treating accident victims, it would seem that the instructor would know best the appropriate skills and knowledge to be learned. But making decisions about what is ideal or what should be is something many programmers shun. They proclaim that their role is one of assessing needs, not determining needs, often without realizing that real needs, those that represent a gap between what is and what should be, cannot be measured even with the most sophisticated needs-assessment tools. Much of continuing education prides itself on being a service field—serving the needs of learners. As Monette (1979) indicates, "There seems to exist in adult education a fear of unmasking the value choices underlying adult educational practice, as if once identified they might prove embarrassing to this 'service-oriented' profession. The belief that adult educators ought not to impose their own educational and curricular values if they can avoid doing so and the fact that adult students can vote with their feet are the two main factors that have parented the 'service orientation' in adult education. . . . The educator is placed in a relatively subservient role, a role which attempts to release him of the ethical burdens involved in defining educational aims by invoking the felt needs of the learners" (p. 87).

Even if program planners want to avoid the burden of making value choices, it is impossible for them to maintain a neutral stance, even if their programming is of the smorgasbord type that attempts to serve solely the interests identified by potential learners. It is impossible to program for all interests that learners identify; indeed, interests identified may be in conflict with each other. The programmer must therefore establish priorities concerning which interest areas to program for and thus is making a value decision.

But back to the dilemma of deciding on "should be" questions and who should be involved in stating them. Freire (1970) has suggested an approach to programming in which the educator is involved with learners in making decisions about needs and programming approaches. Freire says an educational program consists of two phases, (1) thematic research and (2) the educational program. "Thematic investigation will seek to identify significant themes, establish links between themes, and, in the process, pose these themes (with their implied opposites) as problems—all viewed within the historical-cultural context of the people" (Lloyd, 1974, p. 60).

Within the Freirian approach, there is no mention of determining needs as such. "The educational program phase includes making presentations to people in 'circles of culture,' Freire's term for small groups of people (no larger than twenty). The themes drawn from the previous research are posed as questions or problems. In presenting these themes, the educators use visual materials such as slides and photos. They also use newspaper articles, stories, poems, dramatizations, and similar modes for suggesting themes. Within the culture circles, coordinators, who are preferably local persons trained in Freirian methods, lead the discussions" (Apps, 1979, p. 123).

In the Freirian approach, needs are determined as a natural progression of discussion but are prompted by research done by the coordinators and also encouraged by questions the coordinators raise during the discussion process. This discussion process, often seen as controversial, results in consciousness raising —people become aware of their real needs. An outsider does not determine the needs, but the identification is a cooperative effort between educator and learner. The process of need determination is viewed as an educational activity, not as a precursor to an educational program.

Although many questions can be raised about needs and needs assessment, the process remains an important one to many continuing education programmers. As Grabowski (1982) points out: "Needs assessments serve several useful purposes: (1) as starting points for planning, (2) to give a sense of direction, (3) to justify starting or stopping a program, (4) to modify ongoing programs, (5) to evaluate an institution's goals and mission" (p. 60).

There are obvious times when need assessment is vital to continuing education programming—particularly when it relates to programming for learner interests. It is when one attempts to define what the interests of learners are that the various needs-assessment tools are most relevant. But when the programming is concerned with normative needs, other approaches than the traditional needs assessment appear more appropriate. But whether programming for interests or normative needs, the programmer cannot avoid making value decisions. It is impossible for a programmer in continuing education to remain neutral.

2. *Educational outcomes (objectives) must be identified before an educational activity begins.*

We can identify several assumptions implicit in this statement: (1) It is important to know the outcomes of an educational activity before commencing. (2) It is possible to identify educational outcomes. (3) Educational outcomes will remain constant during the course of an educational activity.

Continuing education programmers have been greatly influenced by Tyler's (1950) discussion of objectives. Tyler advised the use of behavioral objectives that could be measured empirically and suggested that such objectives serve both as guides for educational activity and as checkpoints for determining the success of an educational activity. Other authors such as

Mager (1962) have taken a narrower view of behavioral objectives. Mager focused on performance outcomes. Tyler was concerned more broadly with behavioral change, including performance outcomes but also the learner's development of effective ways of thinking, developing social attitudes, acquiring information, and developing appreciations (Tyler, 1950, p. 37).

But not all educators accept Tyler's view on objectives. Many question not only the value of stating educational objectives in behavioral terms (even broad behavioral terms, as Tyler has done) but also whether it makes sense to state educational objectives before an educational activity begins. As Kliebard (1975) writes, "One wonders whether the long-standing insistence by curriculum theorists that the first step in making a curriculum be the specification of objectives has any merit whatsoever. It is even questionable whether stating objectives at all, when they represent external goals allegedly reached through the manipulation of learning experiences, is a fruitful way to conceive of the process of curriculum planning" (p. 80).

Houle (1972) favors the use of educational objectives but concedes that problems may result when a programmer takes an inflexible position toward them. "An objective is a purpose which guides a learner or an educator, not the formal statement of that purpose. Anyone who designs an educational activity may make as clear and exact a forecast as possible of what he hopes to achieve, but the words of that forecast do not capture all his ideas, nor are those ideas the sole determinants of what will occur after the activity begins. He must constantly reshape his plans and procedures in order to come to terms with changes brought about by the desires and abilities of other people or the specific instructional resources he finds available" (pp. 32-33).

Tyler's approach to objectives suggests a close relationship between identified learner needs and the objectives of the program. It only makes sense that this should be so. A need is identified and an educational objective is written to meet the need. But, as Houle (1972) points out, not only do the objectives often change during the course of an educational activity, the learner's needs may change as well. It often happens that once someone learns something, this learning directs the learner in new directions that had not been considered. This, of course, lends some of the excitement to teaching. As Lindeman (1926) warned, "If we enter the discussion with our minds riveted to a preconceived conclusion, the creative spirit will depart from our deliberations; we will come out as we went in, unchanged and unaffected by what might have been a lively cooperative venture. . . . Creativeness is less dependent upon its ends than its means; the creative process, not the created object, is of supreme importance" (pp. 57-59).

Not only did Tyler advocate that educational objectives be written before an educational activity began, but he called for behavioral objectives. "The purpose of a statement of objectives is to indicate the kinds of changes in the student to be brought about so that the instructional activities can be planned and developed in a way likely to attain these objectives; that is, to bring about these changes in students" (Tyler, 1950, p. 45). Thus, for Tyler, education meant a change in students' behavior, and objectives were to be written so that each one specified a particular behavioral change. Many continuing education programmers still follow this basic procedure in writing objectives, although the approach has many critics. Apple and Collins have been particularly critical of programmers who write narrow performance-based behavioral objectives.

Apple (1975), for instance, has written: "The behavioral objectives movement . . . in both its weak and strong senses, has sought to reduce student action to specifiable forms of overt behavior so that the educator can have certitude of outcome. . . . The reductive mentality, one in which the components of cognition are divorced from 'feeling' and can be behaviorally specified, fundamentally misconstrues the nature of human action" (pp. 107, 109).

Collins (1983) states, "According to the behavioristic position, anything that can be meaningfully said about human action can be represented in the form of observational statements. Ideally, these statements constitute precise and measurable observations. Mental constructs, concepts of purpose, and subjective meaning are either reduced to observational statements or are regarded as extraneous mentalistic baggage with no relevance to the real world. To the greatest extent possible, behaviorists have adopted the approach of the natural sciences. In equating human experience with controlled sensory observation, behaviorism shares with the natural sciences the basic philosophic underpinnings of logical positivism" (p. 176).

Given all this, the continuing education programmer is faced with a series of questions: Under what conditions is it appropriate to use educational objectives as a preliminary step in planning educational programs? Under what conditions should educational objectives not be used? When should *performance-based behavioral* objectives be considered? These guidelines seem appropriate: (1) When planning an educational program designed to meet learner needs (learner interests), it is useful to state educational objectives before offering the educational activity. Stating objectives will make the expected outcomes of the educational activity clear to both the learner and the educator. (2) It is appropriate to remain flexible about educational objectives, being willing to change or add new objectives as an educational activity progresses. Changes in learners' interests as an educational program progresses are a convincing argument for changing objectives along the way. (3) It is presumptuous to state specific educational objectives before the beginning of an educational activity in which learners are involved from the outset in identifying their needs (the Freirian approach, for example). In this instance objectives flow naturally out of the educational activity. (4) It would also appear reasonable, during times when learners and educator are intensively involved in an educational activity such as discussed in guideline 3 above, to not take time to identify or write educational objectives. The appropriate action and direction flow naturally out of the educational activity, without the educator or anyone else taking the time to state educational objectives. (5) In some limited situations—for instance, when manual skills are to be learned—it may make sense to state the educational objectives in performance-based behavioral terms. It would seem useful, for example, for an educator to identify in such terms the outcomes of a course designed to teach the operation of shop tools.

3. *A single program development process, with some modifications, will serve all of continuing education.*

Some writers of continuing education materials would ar-

gue that this is false, that there is indeed a considerable diversity
of program planning approaches suggested in the literature. But
let us look more closely. Knowles (1980) lists five phases for developing adult education programs: assessing needs and interests
in program planning, defining purposes and objectives, designing
a comprehensive program, operating a comprehensive program,
and evaluating a comprehensive program. These phases appear
as chapter titles in Knowles's book.

Although Houle (1972) presents a flexible approach to
programming, he identifies the following framework for adult
education programming. He calls the seven phases "decision
points": "1. A possible educational activity is identified, 2. A
decision is made to proceed, 3. Objectives are identified and refined, 4. A suitable format is designed, 5. The format is fitted
into larger patterns of life, 6. The plan is put into effect, 7. The
results are measured and appraised" (p. 47).

Simpson (1982) writes simply: "Organizing and providing
adults with what they want requires: (1) identifying needs, (2)
defining objectives, (3) identifying learning experiences, (4) organizing the experiences into a plan, (5) evaluating outcomes"
(p. 92). And Robinson (1979) says a model for program development should include "Assessment of learner needs (What
does the learner need?), Overall learning goals and design (What
and how will I attempt to teach?), Criteria-evidence (How will I
know I have taught it?), Assess resources (What resources do I
have available for teaching?), Instructional objectives (What
does the learner need to be able to do?) Teaching plan (What
learning experiences need to be provided to accomplish this?)
Evaluation (Did the learner learn?)" (p. 77).

All these models for program development bear a striking
resemblance to Tyler's 1950 curriculum mode, which included
four questions: "(1) What educational purposes should the
school seek to attain? (2) What educational experiences can be
provided that are likely to attain these purposes? (3) How can
these educational experiences be effectively organized? (4) How
can we determine whether these purposes are being attained?"
(pp. 1-2). As we saw, these four questions can be translated
into program-planning phases: (1) identify learner needs, (2) de-

fine objectives, (3) identify learning experiences that meet these objectives, (4) organize learning experiences into an educational plan, and (5) evaluate the outcomes of the educational effort in accordance with the objectives as identified in step 2.

If so many programmers are advocating Tyler's approach to programming for continuing education or some modification of it, why not accept this as an appropriate model? Before answering, let us explore the roots of the model, which will help us understand the assumptions that undergird it. Kliebard (1971) traced Tyler's model for curriculum development to the curriculum work of John Franklin Bobbitt. Bobbitt, in turn, was influenced by Frederick W. Taylor, who had become a spokesperson for scientific management and efficiency in business and industry in the late 1800s. As Kliebard pointed out, "Under Taylor's concept of scientific management, productivity is central and the individual is simply an element in the production system" (p. 76).

The idea of scientific management began to spread throughout society in the late nineteenth and early twentieth centuries, and the public schools searched for applications. "School administrators simply reacted to the influence of the scientific management movement in industry by [extrapolating] those methods to the management of schools. Managers of schools patterned themselves after their counterparts in industry and took pride in adapting the vocabulary and techniques of industry to school administration" (Kliebard, 1971, p. 78). Bobbitt's curriculum work fell in line with the industrial efficiency model, and Tyler's 1950 model became a more modern adaptation. But what problems are there with such an efficiency model as a basis for curriculum design in continuing education? Kliebard argues, "The bureaucratic model, along with its behavioristic and technological refinemenets, threatens to destroy, in the name of efficiency, the satisfaction that one may find in intellectual activity. The sense of delight in intellectual activity is replaced by a sense of urgency. The thrill of the hunt is converted into an efficient kill. The wonder of the journey is superseded by the relentless pursuit of the destination. And to condition the victim to enjoy being conditioned is certainly less humane than open coercion or bribery. The tragic paradox of the production metaphor applied to curriculum is that the dehumanization of education, the alienation of means from ends, the stifling of intellectual curiosity carry with them very few compensations. . . . The particularization of the *educational* product, it turns out, is tantamount to its trivialization" (pp. 91-92).

Kliebard is not alone in his criticism of the Tyler model and those planning models that are offshoots of it. Collins (1983), in a criticism of competency-based education (an educational approach relying on behavioral objectives), writes, "The question which arises . . . concerns the appropriateness of transferring the norms and methods of industry and commerce to other dimensions of human activity. To what extent can we meaningfully apply the notion of units and stages of production in our value-laden educational undertaking? . . . If we are, in effect, moving from a mechanistic, unitized, industrial society to one which increasingly requires relatively quick and intelligent adaptability, it would seem necessary to bring into question the mechanistic nature of the educational infrastructure. Since adults need 'empowerment' to move with confidence between numerous career tasks, the proper emphasis for educators resides in the acts of individuals rather than in the compilation of inert competency statements" (pp. 180-181).

And Huebner (1966) wrote, "Current curricular ideology reflects, almost completely, a technical value system. It has a means-ends rationality that approaches an economic model. End states, end products, or objectives are specified as carefully and as accurately as possible. . . . Major concerns for the curricular worker are the mobilization of material and human resources to produce these ends" (p. 5).

So Tyler's model, with its roots in scientific management and the industrial model, values ends over means, sees inputs as related to outputs, sees measurement of outcome as the important valuation of success for an educational activity. Yet, this is the predominant model that much of the continuing education literature proclaims. One would thus be led to believe that many programmers are following the Tyler approach or some modification of it. One research project suggested otherwise. Pennington and Green (1976) researched program development approaches actually followed by persons developing continuing professional education programs for six professional fields. In summarizing their research, they concluded: "Program development was a form of administrative decision making. Some stimulus from inside or outside of the organization received the attention of a planning agent. The planning agent responded to the stimulus, usually a request or idea for a continuing education activity, in a preliminary fashion to check its strength. If strength of the stimulus was sufficient, resources were gathered to respond. The response took the form of a number of critical decisions and a consideration of alternative activities which would lead to the execution of those decisions that in the end shaped the educational activity" (p. 20).

Pennington and Green evaluated the quality of the planning activity they discovered by comparing the actual programming approaches with the ideal model (the Tyler approach to planning). They discovered that there was little indication of client need analysis, a comprehensive approach to developing objectives was usually missing, few attempts were made to relate selection of teaching methods to learner characteristics, and a comprehensive evaluation did not occur. Yet, all these programs were judged successful. Pennington and Green concluded: "As [the planners] describe their planning actions, it becomes clear that personal values, environmental constraints, available resource alternatives, and other factors impinge on the program development process. These actions have received little attention in the literature but probably represent a major set of critical factors for program development in continuing professional education" (p. 22). It is clear that these programmers were not following Tyler's model to develop their programs, yet many continuing education programmers continue to hold up this model as the ideal.

Considering the arguments just presented, should Tyler's model and its various adaptations be abandoned for an alternative model that continuing education programmers can follow? Or are there instances when that model is appropriate and other instances when an alternative is appropriate? Edelman (1977) argues for multiple realities, "The liberal who perceives public education in America as a liberating influence is offended and threatened by its definition as a form of indoctrination or stultification, though both views are common in popular talk and in academic research. There is evidence of a sort for both perceptions, permitting observation to reflect the presuppositions of the observer. Nietzsche rejected what he called the 'dogma of immaculate perception' " (p. 13). Following Edelman, it makes sense for us not to abandon Tyler and the various adaptations of his planning approach but to realize that multiple realities exist in continuing education programming. Edelman's idea also suggests that we consider quite different approaches to planning.

The writings of Jurgen Habermas (1972) can guide us toward alternative planning approaches. In the previous chapter I pointed out that Habermas saw three approaches to teaching and learning: technical, practical, and emancipatory. Each of these approaches suggests a different perspective on teaching and learning, and likewise these three approaches suggest different perspectives on planning.

Habermas's first category, the technical, which relates to how one controls and manipulates one's environment, would be well served by following Tyler's approach or one of its adaptations. Habermas's second category, which he calls "practical" but which refers to deriving meaning from situations, may be best served by a planning approach considerably different from Tyler's. In an earlier work (Apps, 1979), I discussed what I called a liberal education planning approach. One example I shared was this: "The instructor organizes the course and orders the books, the course is promoted in the community, and if the minimum number of students enrolls, the course is taught. There are no elaborate needs-determination procedures. Nor is there a systematic attempt to involve the anticipated learners in the planning of the course, although some of this is often done informally so that the curriculum planner can get some feel for the potential students' interests. Plainly and simply, someone decides to teach something, it is promoted, and then it is taught" (p. 131).

Following this approach or some adaptation of it, little attention is paid to an elaborate system with stages and phases, although there is some structure. What is important is that it provides opportunities for learners who want to interact with other learners about a topic of mutual interest. They care not where the discussion will take them: They are as interested in the journey as in the destination.

It is Habermas's third category, emancipatory education, that we see least often reflected in planning approaches. As I pointed out in the previous chapter, emancipatory learning has a critical, an integrative, and an action perspective. It is concerned with empowering learners, not only with providing them with information or attempting to change their behavior in a narrow, predefined sense.

Freire's approach to teaching learning and programming (although he does not use those words) comes closest, in my judgment to offering what Habermas calls emancipatory education. The assumptions of Freire's approach are these:

1. Education is never neutral . . . [it] either helps people liberate themselves or it contributes to their loss of freedom and humanity.
2. Human beings are free to act on their world. . . .
3. The focus of education includes changing the structure of society as well as the social situations in which people live. In this process, individuals themselves change. . . .
4. The approach to dealing with societal problems should be dialectical. . . .
5. The process of education is holistic . . . one does not first do some type of survey to determine needs, then write learning objectives, then plan learning experiences, and so on. . . .
6. Knowledge occurs in the process basically through two reciprocally related activities . . . in the process of responding to problems, specific knowledge—research information, facts, ideas, opinions of outside resource people—is needed. In addition, the participants' own experience, brought to awareness through the

reflection and problem-posing process, constitutes a major source of knowledge. . . .
7. The educator who follows the Freire approach
is a facilitator who guides but does not direct,
who is more concerned to raise questions than
to provide answers (Apps, 1979, pp. 123-125).

On the basis of this discussion, what guidelines can we
offer programmers?

First, programmers should recognize that varying purposes for continuing education suggest varying programming
approaches. For instance, it may be appropriate to follow Tyler's model for programs in which specific knowledge and skills
are to be learned, as in some career development education, and
for programs that are developed to serve learner interests. But
for programs designed with liberal arts as content—music, literature, art—a programming approach less structured and less concerned for identified end products would be more appropriate.
And in areas like community development, where a concern is
often the empowerment of learners, still another approach to
programming ought to be considered. Earlier I suggested Freire's
approach as one alternative in such situations.

A second suggestion is to continue to program creatively,
as many programmers do. Although Tyler's approach has provided a useful theoretical base for some types of continuing
education programming, it has also inhibited creative programmers. By implication, the continuing education literature, with
few exceptions, has suggested that there is a "right" way to program—there must be a needs assessment and analysis, there must
be educational objectives, learning experiences must be designed
to meet these objectives, and so on. Creative programmers have
been thwarted in developing programming approaches that fit
their own situations. Yet, those successful programmers will try
new approaches, and one day these approaches may become a
part of the literature of continuing education programming.

By following the guidelines for critical, synoptic, and normative analysis as illustrated here, practitioners can examine in
depth the programming approaches they use. In critical analysis,

practitioners identify assumptions, metaphors, and slogans that are parts of their programming language. With critical analysis, practitioners can peel back the layers of words that sometimes obscure the meaning of what they do.

In synoptic analysis, practitioners examine program development and research and become aware of the divergent positions concerning such ideas as needs, objectives, and needs assessment.

And in normative analysis, practitioners make decisions about what they believe program approaches should be. These decisions are based on earlier critical and synoptic analysis. From such analyses, practitioners can begin to feel empowered in their role as programmers. They can become confident that their programming efforts are based on their own analysis and that they are not relying solely on what some "expert" has suggested is the proper approach.

With continuing education practitioners taking charge of both the practice and theory of programming, the field will be presented with a rich array of programming theory and practice. Not only will the collection of "tried and true" practical approaches be expanded, but the theoretical underpinnings of these approaches will be expanded as well. These are some of the potential outcomes when practitioners do critical, synoptic, and normative analysis of their programming approaches.

Summary

This chapter has been concerned with content for continuing education programs and program development approaches. To illustrate how one might analyze key positions about content and program development, I have combined critical, synoptic, and normative approaches into one integrated approach. In previous chapters where analysis has been illustrated, I have treated them as discrete approaches. In this chapter and the one following, I identify and examine assumptions, metaphors, and slogans (critical analysis), share ideas from the literature (synoptic analysis), and develop some thoughts about what ought to be (normative analysis) without trying to separate the approaches. Most practitioners, when they do analysis following the suggestions in this book, will integrate critical, synoptic, and normative approaches. In this chapter I have illustrated how one might do this.

Three belief statements related to content for continuing education were analyzed: (1) Continuing education is transferring information from a source or depository (an educator, book, videotape, and so on) to a learner. (2) Society is experiencing an information explosion, making the task of continuing education increasingly more difficult. (3) The only information worthy of inclusion in an educational program is that which can be traced to an expert or to scientific research. Concerning content, I offered these guidelines for the continuing education programmer: Be open to a wide range of content, from a multitude of sources, and realize that an education program is more than delivering information to learners.

Likewise, I examined three beliefs about continuing education programming approaches: (1) Continuing education programs should be based on needs. (2) Educational outcomes (objectives) must be identified before an educational activity begins. (3) A single program development process, with some modifications, will serve all of continuing education. For the continuing education programmer, I offered these guidelines: First, recognize that the varying purposes for continuing education suggest varying programming approaches. Tyler's approach to programming (or one of its adaptations) cannot serve all the purposes of continuing education, particularly those purposes designed to provide emancipatory education. For emancipatory education, Freirian approaches are more appropriate. Second, continue to program creatively, fitting programming approaches to particular situations and purposes. Attempting to fit a single programming approach to all programming may be more of a problem than following no programming approach at all.

9

Rethinking Priorities in
Continuing Education

〰〰〰〰〰〰〰〰〰〰〰〰〰〰〰〰

In our various roles as instructors, programmers, or administrators of continuing education we are obligated to follow one policy or another. Many of us also have responsibility for writing policy statements. In this chapter we will explore the analysis of policy in continuing education from two perspectives: (1) approaches to analyzing existing policy statements and (2) challenges for those who develop policy for continuing education. Before going on, though, let us define *policy*. Jantsch (1975) said, "A policy is a set of principles laid out for the purpose of regulating simultaneously and in a viable mode a multitude of interacting relationships pertaining to many qualities and dimensions of human life—in short, a theme underlying a life" (p. 6).

Key phrases in Jantsch's definition are *regulating simultaneously* and *interacting relationships*. Let us return to the metaphor of the stream, introduced in Chapter One, to grasp the meaning of these words. In Chapter One I compared the continuing education practitioner to a canoeist paddling in an ever-changing stream, encountering obstacles usually without warning, and trying always to keep the canoe afloat and headed

189

downstream. Jantsch also uses a stream metaphor to discuss policy: "There are many forces acting in the stream, pulling and pushing from all sides, sometimes mutually enhancing or canceling out, but more often conflicting with each other in complex ways" (Jantsch, 1975, p. 6). Policy helps keep us in the stream and moving. We can visualize the two sides of the stream representing opposing positions as we steer a course. These opposing positions might include a behavioral perspective versus a humanistic perspective, emphasis on vocational training versus emphasis on liberal education, institutionally sponsored continuing education versus self-directed learning, economic survival versus high-risk programs, and so on.

Sometimes, as we move downstream, we may find it more comfortable to put our continuing education craft ashore and subscribe to one or another of the positions mentioned. In so doing we avoid the tension of steering a course in the swift current. From time to time we may find it necessary to spend some time on shore, to catch our breath and make future plans. But if we stay on shore too long, if we subscribe to a particular position that bridles our thinking, we become stagnant. Eventually we must enter the stream again. Just as the stream provides different conditions as it flows, so does continuing education. Thus there is a need to constantly appraise policy and revise or develop new policy positions.

As is evident from the metaphor of the canoeist paddling in a stream, an ideal state is seldom reached. One is constantly steering a course between what appear to be opposing positions, and one is always trying to avoid obstacles in the water. But policy keeps us participating, keeps continuing education a vital part of human activity.

Examining Policy Statements

Analyzing a policy statement can help us more fully understand it as well as assist us in determining whether it requires updating. The analysis can follow the same procedures introduced previously in this book: searching for assumptions and questioning them, identifying slogans and metaphors, and so on.

Let us turn to a specific policy statement and illustrate, by example, one approach to analysis. The statement is from the 1983 Blue Ribbon Commission Report on Education in America titled *A Nation at Risk: The Imperative for Educational Reform* (National Commission on Excellence in Education, 1983): "In a world of ever-accelerating competition and change in conditions in the workplace, of ever-greater danger, and of ever-larger opportunities for those prepared to meet them, educational reform should focus on the goal of creating a learning society. At the heart of such a society is the commitment to a set of values and to a system of education that affords all members the opportunity to stretch their mind to full capacity, from early childhood through adulthood, learning more as the world itself changes" (p. 13).

What assumptions are suggested by this passage?

1. The workplace is increasingly more competitive.
2. Educational reform should focus on having everyone learn.
3. Learning is something that can be accumulated.
4. There is a limit to the capacity of the mind.
5. Learning will help us cope with ever-accelerating competition, workplace change, danger, and ever-larger opportunities.
6. Education should be provided from early childhood through adulthood.
7. A single set of basic values about learning should undergird a society in which everyone is learning.

If we would agree that these are reasonable assumptions to be derived from this passage, which might we question?

Assumption 1: Is the workplace increasingly more competitive? What about the efforts in Japan and in this country toward making the workplace more cooperative? What about the many self-employed people, for many of whom the workplace is their home and they are the sole employee? Is the workplace increasingly more competitive for them?

Assumption 2: Is it possible that large numbers of people in our society are not learning? Or is the implication that large numbers of adults are not participating in sponsored continuing education programs? It seems logical to believe that, for survival alone, all of us must and do continue to learn. But there is obviously a difference between learning by oneself and learning in a sponsored continuing education activity. Is it necessary that everyone participate in sponsored continuing education?

Assumption 3: Is learning something that one accumulates throughout life? In what ways is learning more profound than incremental accumulation? How can learning involve new frontiers of understanding, new perspectives, deeper values? Does not learning often involve unlearning, when we shed old ways of viewing, old values and beliefs? Is learning something better described in terms of quality than of quantity?

Assumption 4: Does the mind have limits? Can we reach a point where no more learning can occur, when our mind is full and will hold no more? Most of us, I believe, would subscribe to a belief that there is no limit to learning, although as we age, some types of learning may be more difficult than others.

What metaphors can be found in the passage from *A Nation at Risk*? One interesting metaphor in the passage is "stretch one's mind." This metaphor suggests an image of a rubber band. We visualize the mind as a rubber band, stretching further and further, until it will not stretch anymore and it snaps. Is this the image we wish to portray about the human mind?

Many policy statements in continuing education contain slogans, and this one is no exception. "Creating a learning society" is expressed as a goal of educational reform. Creating a learning society has been a continuing education slogan for years. We see it appearing in legislative and other policy statements from time to time, but what does it mean, and what is the purpose for using it?

At one level the slogan means we should concentrate on providing educational opportunity for all ages, young and old, and that it is the responsibility of our nation to provide such opportunity. At another level the slogan is a rallying cry that we should all continue to make a conscious attempt to keep learning and that unless we do keep learning, something drastic is likely to happen to us. At still another level, the slogan makes no sense. We are all learning, every day—it is a necessary part of our continued existence. It is illogical to suggest that we become a part of a learning society when we are already a learning society.

Of course, each of these perspectives could be defended. The writer of the slogan in the context of this particular policy statement could argue that the meaning of the slogan was to focus on increased attention to organized learning, not the learning that all of us do as a part of living. And the critic could question whether organized, institutionally sponsored learning is the appropriate form of continuing education for all learners.

Analysis of policy statements can help us see the variety of points of view inherent in them as well as help us understand not only what the policy statement seems to say but what is sometimes hidden within the words.

Issues for Policy Makers

As one might suspect, writing policy statements is not an easy task. Here I concentrate on two areas of challenge for policy makers: (1) challenges surrounding the process of developing policy statements and (2) areas in which new policy should be developed for continuing education.

Concerns for Developing Policy. In developing policy, one must draw from a wide assortment of information sources. A narrow approach to policy development is to rely on the statistics of the recent past and make numerical projections into the future as the major basis for policy formulation. Few policy developers follow this approach these days, because too many factors affect projections of enrollment statistics, budget, and population characteristics.

Today's policy developer relies on statistics but draws on a much broader base of information. Sociology, psychology, history, anthropology, and philosophy can all contribute to developing policy statements. The actual process of policy development combines analysis with intuition, relying on both, but does not give precedence to either. The policy maker today is grounded in the specifics of practice in continuing education, but he or she is not influenced only by the "what is" and is constantly searching for "what might be." To reflect once more on the analogy of the stream, the continuing education policy maker is constantly striving to steer a course that keeps continuing education in the stream and moving, conscious always of the pressures that are ever present.

The continuing education policy maker is at the same time a realist and an idealist. As Jantsch (1975) eloquently argues, "I believe that there exists an urgent need to explore the dynamics of those areas 'beyond the clouds,' where human cultures are rooted and from where *cultural change* emanates as the powerful guiding factor of social and individual change. In attempting this task, I took equally seriously all modes of holistic insight: paradigms of physical and social science, artistic expression, mystical insight, and psychic revelatory processes" (p. xv).

One must be particularly mindful of the metaphors one uses in writing policy statements. Currently policy makers (all the rest of us, too) are caught up in using military metaphors. World Wars I and II, Korea, Vietnam, and the host of other conflagrations since have militarized our language. *Cutting edge,* a term often used (as in "the cutting edge of continuing education research"), is a military term. We talk about continuing education organizations having staff and line and a chain of command. We develop strategy and tactics. We talk of "strategic planning" and sometimes even title our policy statements with those words (*A Strategic Plan for the Future*). When we hire a staff member, we often say the person has come on board, as if he or she had joined the navy and gone to sea. We discharge employees, we identify the need for "breakthroughs," and so on.

But why not continue to use military language in our policy statements? People understand the meaning of the words, and is not communication of prime concern in any written statement? Of course communication (understanding) is essential in any policy statement, but what are we communicating when we use military metaphors? By using military metaphors in writing policy statements, we leave the impression (hidden, to be sure, in most instances) that in continuing education, as in the military, there are winners and there are losers. Some learners win, some lose; some educational programs win, some lose; some programmers win and some lose, and so on. Is this the impression we wish to convey? By focusing on winning and losing as a dichotomy, we offer a limited view of problems and situations. Is not continuing education often exploring, examining, and dreaming, rather than winning or losing? Is not learning something more profound than winning or losing? Do we want our policy statements to include language and the concepts to which the language relates that are so limiting?

According to Peters and Waterman (1982), the business world is developing new metaphors, "which do open up rich [ways] for thinking about managing—however threatening they may be to executives steeped in the old school" (p. 101). These metaphors include sailing, playfulness, seesaws, space stations, and garbage cans. What are the metaphors for a new continuing education? What metaphors will take us into the future and inspire us rather than constrain us? Military and technology metaphors constrain us. I have just explored some military metaphors. Some commonly used metaphors from technology are "the brain as computer," "inputs and outputs," and "gearing up."

Perhaps, as the anthropologist Clifford Geertz (1983) suggests, the time has come to begin blurring genres—that is, drawing more widely for our metaphors. He suggests we look to the humanities as one important source. By doing so, we can begin to view metaphors that are dramatically different from those with science and technology roots. We can view an anecdote or someone's story as a metaphor for understanding. (For instance, the old drama metaphor "All the world's a stage" can be explored.) We can search for metaphors that evoke feeling as well as understanding.

A metaphor can help people see in new ways. "What they see and how they see are greatly dependent on the way the materials of a given work are formed. Under the guidance of form, those who read or look or listen attentively can create new orders within themselves. Doing so, they are likely to discover new meanings, unsuspected angles of vision; they may discover original perceptions of what it is like to be alive, 'themes of relevance' against which students can pose worthwhile questions" (Greene, 1973, p. 16). Thus the metaphors we use in our policy statements and the way the statements are written can have a powerful effect on those who read them.

As Murchland (1982) explained, a severe problem we have in society is "linguistic failure—a void between what is said and what is meant, an inability to produce effective metaphors, a lag between events and our capacity to exercise symbolic control over them" (p. 303).

Those of us who write continuing education policy are challenged to use language that liberates rather than confines, that communicates rather than confuses, that shows direction for the future rather than rationalizes the present. The metaphors we use thus become key to our communication.

When writing policy statements, one must also realize that the activity is never completed. As conditions change, so must the policy statement. The wisdom the policy maker must possess is knowing that conditions have changed and being aware when present policy is outdated and does not reflect these changes.

Policy Challenges. What are some areas in which new policy in continuing education should be developed? The following are beginning places:

1. The need for vision in continuing education.
2. The need to develop a critical attitude.
3. The need to develop policies about aims for continuing education.
4. The need to develop policies that relate continuing education to other facets of education.
5. The need for policy statements that illustrate a broadened view of how and where continuing education takes place.

1. *The need for vision in continuing education.* For more than fifty years leaders in the continuing education movement spent much of their time trying to convince the public that

adults could learn and that educating adults was an important activity. Much energy of these charismatic leaders in the field was devoted to traveling the country appearing at workshops and conferences, speaking to business and industry groups, and writing articles and books that spread "the gospel" of continuing education.

This was particularly true for many educators of adults who were associated with colleges and universities. But this is a new time for the field of continuing education. Those who teach, administer, and make policy for continuing education ask for much more today than pronouncements glorifying the virtues of continuing education in abstract, general terms. Those in continuing education, particularly adult learners, are interested in future direction. They are looking for vision. Naisbitt (1982) writes, "Too often a shared vision or purpose is absent" (p. 94). All segments of society, including education, are caught up in the present, with little concern or at least little attention given to a decade ahead. Naisbitt believes that our society is moving toward more long-term concerns and this shift will affect education. "The short-term to long-term shift will transform the way you look at education and employment. The notion of lifelong learning is already replacing the short-term approach to education, whereby you went to school, graduated, and that was that. . . . The long-range perspective may signal the need to return to the idea of a generalist education. If you specialize too much, you may find your specialty becoming obsolete in the long run. As a generalist, committed to lifelong education, you can change with the times" (Naisbitt, 1982, pp. 95–96).

At the present time, though, with much of continuing education, particularly that which is tax-supported, under careful scrutiny by decision makers, much energy goes toward evaluation and accountability. Evaluation as a process has been elevated to mystical levels in recent years as many continuing education programs strive to endure. This is particularly so for tax-supported programs offered by the Cooperative Extension Service, college and university general extension programs, vocational/technical school programs, and programs offered by public schools and community colleges. How-to workshops on evaluation have sprung up in many areas, attracting programmers and administrators searching for magical pieces of evidence to convince those holding the purse strings that their programs are worthy of continuing.

In the extreme, some continuing education programmers become so influenced by evaluation and programming for "impact" that they make program decisions based on "potential for impact" rather than basing programs on a host of other criteria such as worthwhileness, developing a sense of humanness, or focusing on a controversial issue or some community problem.

That is not to say that evaluation and accountability are not important to consider. Few educators would say they are not, but how important are they? And to what extent does continuing education languish in the present, trying to convince decision makers of its importance rather than projecting ahead?

Many decision makers, however, are looking for hints of vision, new ideas, new programs, and evidence of risk taking. But many educators of adults believe their task is to convince these decision makers that what they have been doing all along is what matters, if they could only figure out a way to put the accomplishments into a form that decision makers could better understand.

Even when the new approaches are developed for communicating continuing education activity, many educators of adults have spent so much time evaluating that they have nothing worthwhile to communicate. They have spent their time developing accountability and reporting approaches and have overlooked the most important thing they could do—developing a vision for the future and acting on it.

Critical, synoptic, and particularly normative analysis as discussed in this book can help the continuing education practitioner develop a vision for the future. By carefully examining one's present practice (critical analysis), by exploring the breadth of alternatives (synoptic analysis), and then by considering "what should be" questions (normative analysis), the practitioner is well on the way toward developing a vision.

2. *The need to develop a critical attitude.* Along with developing a vision, all of us in continuing education must develop

a critical attitude toward the field and everything it comprises. Policy makers, particularly, must develop a critical view of everything they write.

By *critical attitude* I mean questioning the worth of what we do, the methods we use to plan and to teach, the assumptions we hold about adults as learners, and the purposes of continuing education activity. As Lyons (1982) wrote, "The point is to recall us to the labor of really trying to find out what is the true picture or the best way of doing something, especially as regards those things over which we have some control and which closely affect our fellow humans" (p. 229).

This entire book has focused on developing a critical attitude toward continuing education, including ways of doing critical analysis of various facets of the field. A challenge to the continuing education policy maker is to incorporate a critical attitude in policy statements.

3. *The need to develop policies about aims for continuing education.* As discussed in Chapter Six, we are experiencing major shifts in society. Are we prepared to develop new aims for continuing education? Are we in continuing education open to encouraging, as an aim, cultural criticism that may lead to social change? Is it appropriate for continuing education to aim toward influencing the direction of social change rather than merely responding to the changes after they have occurred? This is a major policy question, requiring discussion and debate. As Brameld (1965) wrote, many people hold the view that educational agencies "are primarily agents to carry out the orders of the power constellations that are already heavily entrenched in controlling economic, political, and military policies. In this case, they consider their primary obligation to be one of allegiance to those policies. Or, they may accept the alternative view that the basic purpose of education is to teach . . . people how to become their own masters in practice as well as in theory—in short, to take control of the local, national, and international community rather than to let the community take control of them" (p. 8).

Few policy statements speak of education for social change or education for emancipation, as discussed in Chapter

Seven. Too often the policy statements, either directly or by implication, suggest a passive role for continuing education. Continuing education helps people prepare for jobs, helps them adjust to problems, helps them acquire literacy skills. "All of this assumes a passive, conservative role for continuing education. At most, cheer people on, provide skills for what is inevitable. There is little possibility for social or personal change. The goal of adulthood is merely to survive" (Zwerling, 1982, p. 49).

It is logical that aims for continuing education be broad and include several dimensions, yet present-day aims lack the vision of encouraging people to take charge of their own lives, their communities, and their government. Many continuing education programs claim they provide basic, or literacy, education. Often this means literacy education in the narrow sense, helping people learn a second language or develop basic reading, writing, and number skills. Literacy education can be viewed more broadly and with vision. Literacy education can include political literacy—providing an understanding and appreciation of government and political decision making; historical literacy—providing an understanding and appreciation of history and the lessons of the past; ethical and moral literacy—providing an understanding of ethics and ethical decision making; and humanistic literacy—developing an understanding of what it means to be human.

If continuing education agencies and institutions and providers in general have problems in determining far-reaching aims, college and university continuing education in particular has its own set of problems. With the great increase in continuing education providers during the past decade, much of college and university continuing education accepted that it must compete with these providers. The fastest-growing area of continuing education is business and industry, and thus higher education has viewed corporate educators as major competitors. As Ernest Boyer, former U.S. Commissioner of Education and president of the Carnegie Foundation, warns, "Can the colleges and universities fulfill their unique role in society and do more than respond to the latest marketplace demands? The danger is that, in a bid for survival, higher education will seek to imitate its rivals . . . confronting competition, some campuses have become consumer-driven enterprises, following the marketplace and constantly juggling programs to meet new demands" (1983, p. 32).

In the parlance of continuing education, we call this "programming to meet the needs of the clientele." Some continuing education programmers would argue that unless they developed programs to "meet the needs" of those living in their communities, they would have to close their doors. But as Boyer exclaims, "Survival without a sense of mission is hardly preferable to extinction; indeed, it may be the forerunner of extinction. The ultimate loser would be a society no longer able to count on the cement that keeps it from falling apart, with people scattered into myriad unrelated cells, trained but not educated, sure of the individual person's special desires and interests but ignorant of shared purposes and ideals" (p. 32).

In addition to competition from other continuing education providers, another dimension of the problem with college and university continuing education, in some ways an opposite situation, is the need for higher education to purge itself of those programming approaches that appear nontraditional and different from what is perceived as the primary thrust of higher education—educating the full-time degree-seeking student. Daloz (1983) believes that much of higher education is moving toward the 1950s rather than toward the twenty-first century. "It is unfortunate . . . that rather than moving ahead and attempting to invent new institutions to suit a transformed environment, we are moving backward, getting rid of all but the most senior and traditional faculty members, and frequently mutilating the very programs—the external degree programs, the special services for new learners, the 'experiential assessment' components—that could keep our institutions alive. . . . The problem, say the professors, is that the new programs lack quality. The solution, echo the administrators, is 'quality control' " (p. 34).

Extension and continuing education programs are often caught up in this purgir ʒ of programs deemed to be of low quality. College and university continuing education programs seem damned if they do and damned if they do not. What is a middle ground, what aims should college and university continuing education pursue? Are there unique aims for these programs that are not competitive with the aims of other continuing education providers, particularly business and industry? And, at the same time, are there aims that will satisfy and be consistent with the broader aims of higher education? This is a major issue that policy makers in continuing education are wrestling with these days. What are some of the choices?

Continuing education can program in the area of controversial issues and will face little competition from other continuing education providers, particularly business and industry. Major exceptions are various women's groups and other organizations that program almost exclusively with certain social issues. These groups generally advocate a certain social position, such as nuclear disarmament or passage of the Equal Rights Amendment, while higher-education-sponsored programs usually attempt to provide more than one side to an issue, leaving the decision-making responsibility up to the persons who attend.

Continuing education can explore content areas in greater depth and in a different way than business and industry providers. As Boyer (1983) explains, "Companies cannot and will not go to the heart of education. Industry education, with all its variety, is not likely to achieve the kind of understanding that can result when students and teachers come together to test ideas, reflect upon deeper meanings, and weigh alternative conclusions. Through such encounters information is placed in a larger context and the relationship of knowledge of life's dilemmas can be thoughtfully explored" (p. 38). In addition, college and university continuing education can offer such programs as reading for understanding, thinking creatively as well as rationally, exploring literature and poetry, can present programs in music and art and thus provide an opportunity for examining esthetics, ethics, and morality—topics that few non–higher education providers include. (There are exceptions—libraries often sponsor discussions of great works of literature, museums offer programs to understand and appreciate art works, and so on).

College and university continuing education can also program in public policy in at least two dimensions. At one time, the public service dimension of many higher education institutions included working with government leaders in drafting public policy statements that often became law. An early activity of University of Wisconsin Extension professors was to work with state legislators in drafting state legislation (Carstensen, 1981). Such activity, though somewhat diminished during the last several decades, remains a unique contribution that college and university continuing education can make to public policy.

Another contribution continuing education can make is sponsoring educational programs on public policy issues. Paul Hadley of the University of Southern California states: "My definition of the role of continuing education and extension would include a very heavy responsibility in the field of public opinion and public participation in issues of public policy. I think that continuing educators are indeed the indicated persons in the university and perhaps also in the community to provide forums for the free exchange of information and opinions" (quoted in Morrison, 1979, p. 6).

It is critical that continuing education policy makers wrestle with the aims for the field and clearly communicate these to the public. This is particularly so for college and university continuing education programs. The question "What is unique about college and university education programs?" must be answered.

Following the approaches to analysis suggested on these pages can help the practitioner examine, seek alternatives, and make decisions about future directions for continuing education.

4. *The need to develop policies that relate continuing education to other facets of education.* Many educators of adults have argued for a discrete continuing education, to illustrate that it is profoundly different from elementary and secondary education and even higher education. This has proved to be a shortsighted position and one that must be corrected as continuing education looks forward. Because there are differences between children and adults, some adult educators have deduced that all educational programs must also be different.

Knowles (1980) has led this discussion with his idea of andragogy, the education of adults, in contrast with pedagogy, the education of children.

Nell Keddie (1980), of the Department of Extra-Mural Studies, University of London, argues that continuing education is more like the rest of the educational system than different from it. "Adult educators commonly claim a distinctive nature for their enterprise, implying that adult education differs significantly from the rest of the educational system. This claim refers to its diversity of forms, its voluntary nature, and its concern with meeting individual need through a student-centered curriculum. The current preoccupation with professionalization also emphasizes the claim that the education of adults requires distinctive teaching skills" (p. 45).

Keddie argues that continuing education's concern for the individual learner is similar to the concern of many primary school teachers and particularly remedial teachers in secondary schools. "Both adult educators and primary teachers not only see education as person-centered rather than subject-centered but also tend to value pedagogic skills above academic qualifications" (p. 47). Keddie also points out that, like elementary education, adult education is primarily concerned with cultural reproduction, rather than education that is designed to be critical and questioning.

Although there are important differences between education designed for children and education designed for adults (see Chapters Five, Six, and Seven particularly), there are nevertheless many similarities that continuing education has so far all but ignored. An interesting and important exception is the way much of continuing education has taken Ralph Tyler's approach to school curriculum design as a model for designing educational programs for adults. For instance, many of the curriculum questions raised by such writers as Kliebard (1971, 1975) and Apple (1975) can be applied to the development of curriculum for continuing education. Basic learning theory such as the theories described in Bigge (1976) have application to adult learning. Fundamental discussions about the nature of human beings such as the work of Greene (1973) have application to adults as they do to children.

From discussions with elementary, secondary, and higher education representatives, much useful information and insight can be gained. What are the characteristics of today's secondary and postsecondary students, the persons who will participate in continuing education classes, courses, and workshops in a few years? What are their expectations, what teaching approaches have worked well with them, what are their attitudes toward learning? Likewise, educators of adults can tell educators in the schools the particular difficulties they have seen adults in their programs facing.

Policy makers can help ensure that these discussions take place, by recommending that educators of adults talk with elementary teachers from time to time and even, perhaps, that elementary and secondary educators have the opportunity for part-time teaching in continuing education programs. Although this practice takes place today, some educators of adults do not support the idea because "those people are not trained for educating adults." With some assistance, any deficiency these elementary and secondary educators may have in working with adults will be overcome. Discussions with these part-time teachers about the nature of the adult learners they are facing could have a profound effect on the way these teachers work with children as well as on the curriculum of childhood education. Although much continuing education takes place in settings quite different from those of elementary, secondary, and higher education (much is similar, too), all adults have had considerable experience in schools.

There is still another reason that we in continuing education should be interested in elementary and secondary education particularly. The reason could be looked on as self-protecting. Elementary and secondary education has been severely criticized in recent years, and when one element of education is criticized, in the minds of many, all of education shares the criticism. The criticisms have been far-reaching. As Mortimer Adler (1982) said, "We are all sufferers from our continued failure to fulfill the educational obligations of a democracy. We are all the victims of a school system that has only gone halfway along the road to realize the promise of democracy" (p. 4).

Norman Cousins, former editor of the *Saturday Review,*

described the current graduates of our colleges and universities this way: "We are turning out young men and women who are superbly trained but poorly educated. They are a how-to generation, less concerned with the nature of things than with the working of things. They are beautifully skilled but intellectually underdeveloped. They know everything that is to be known about the functional requirements of their trade but very little about the human situation that serves as the context for their work. They have been separated from tradition and from the creative splendor accumulated over the years by gifted minds. They live without allusion" (1983, p. 4).

Thus for at least two reasons we must be concerned with the happenings in elementary, secondary, and higher education. By virtue of having the word *education* in the title of our field, when various facets of education are criticized, we by association are also criticized. It matters not that we wish to disclaim any ties to these forms of education known, usually pejoratively, as schooling. And, second, those of us who work as practitioners in continuing education will eventually see the results of schooling in our workshops and classes. We must be concerned about these students' preparation.

5. *The need for policy statements that illustrate a broadened view of how and where continuing education takes place.* Educational technologist Charles Wedemeyer writes, "If learning occurs outside the environment of the school and does not always occur within it, then we must question the assumption (a given in our culture) that specified place, time, and environmental conditions are essential for learning. If learning can and does occur anywhere, any time, under apparently random environmental conditions, then perhaps some of the effort we put into creating special environments for learning may not be necessary" (1981, p. 29).

Wedemeyer raises an important question, for we in continuing education have put considerable emphasis on the environment for learning. Often we deny the existence of, or at least give little importance to, that learning which is called self-directed. Yet, as Tough (1971) has discovered, more than 80 percent of the adults he researched planned at least one learning project during the year he contacted them. Self-directed learning occurs in the home, in the workplace, at a vacation setting, in a library, and in many other places.

As discussed in Chapter Seven, the home computer offers the opportunity for even greater amounts of self-directed learning. The need still exists, though, for the entire field of continuing education, including that segment represented by the more traditional providers, to recognize the value of self-directed learning, often as a useful alternative to attending courses and classes sponsored by a college or university, a technical school, or business and industry. If we indeed are striving toward emancipatory learning, then we must be open to accepting people learning in a variety of ways and in a variety of places. And our policies should reflect this acceptance.

Lindeman ([1926] 1961) reminded us that education is life, yet we value most that education which can be counted and recorded and symbolized with a credential. Some of us may give a nodding acceptance to life experience as education but continue to ask for the credential. Some of us work under the assumption that formally acquired learning is superior to learning acquired through experience and that unless a teacher is involved (other than the learner), the learning is somehow suspect.

We have a considerable distance to go in accepting the variety of approaches to continuing education; in fact, we have difficulty agreeing on what exactly counts as legitimate learning. The dilemma of defining what is continuing education and where it occurs is proving to be one of the most provocative challenges for continuing education policy makers.

Summary

Policy is defined as a regulator of human activity. Most of us, from time to time, are involved in making policy decisions. All of us who work in continuing education are faced with carrying out policy.

Policy statements can be analyzed following procedures similar to those for analyzing other facets of continuing education. One can identify assumptions, search for slogans and metaphors, and raise questions about all three. One can search for alternatives, and one can advocate a particular policy.

Challenges for continuing education policy makers include challenges for the writing process (draw from a wide variety of sources for information, and be particularly mindful of the metaphors used); the need for vision in continuing education; the need to develop a critical attitude; the need to develop policies about aims for continuing education; the need to develop policies that relate continuing education to other facets of education; and the need for policy statements that illustrate a broadened view of how and where continuing education takes place.

References

Adams, F. *Unearthing Seeds of Fire: The Idea of Highlander.* Winston-Salem, N.C.: John Blair, 1975.

Adler, M. *The Paideia Proposal: An Educational Manifesto.* New York: Macmillan, 1982.

Alinsky, S. *Rules for Radicals: A Primer for Realistic Radicals.* New York: Vintage Books, 1971.

Allport, G. *Becoming.* New Haven, Conn.: Yale University Press, 1955.

Anderson, R. E., and Darkenwald, G. G. *Participation and Persistence in American Adult Education.* New York: College Entrance Examination Board, 1979.

Apple, M. "The Adequacy of Systems Management Procedures in Education." In R. A. Smith (ed.), *Regaining Educational Leadership.* New York: Wiley, 1975.

Apple, M. *Ideology and Curriculum.* London: Routledge & Kegan Paul, 1979.

Apps, J. W. *Toward a Working Philosophy of Adult Education.* Syracuse, N.Y.: Syracuse University Publications in Continuing Education, 1973.

Apps, J. W. *Problems in Continuing Education.* New York: McGraw-Hill, 1979.

Apps, J. W. *The Adult Learner on Campus.* Chicago: Follett, 1981.

209

Apps, J. W. *Improving Your Writing Skills.* Chicago: Follett, 1982.

Apps, J. W. *Characteristics and Problems of Older Returning Students.* Research Division Monograph. Madison: College of Agricultural and Life Sciences, University of Wisconsin, forthcoming.

Aslanian, C. B., and Brickell, H. M. *Americans in Transition.* New York: College Entrance Examination Board, 1980.

Baltes, P. B., and Schaie, K. W. "The Myth of the Twilight Years." *Psychology Today,* March 1974, pp. 35–40.

Barnett, P. *Tools of Thought.* Cambridge: Schenkman, 1981.

Bell, D. "The Social Framework of the Information Society." In M. Dertouszos and J. Moses (Eds.), *The Computer Age: A Twenty-Year View.* Cambridge: MIT Press, 1980.

Bem, D. J. *Beliefs, Attitudes, and Human Affairs.* Monterey, Calif.: Brooks/Cole, 1970.

Bergevin, P. *A Philosophy for Adult Education.* New York: Seabury Press, 1967.

Berry, W. "People, Land, and Community." *Sierra,* September/October 1983, pp. 48–52.

Bigge, M. L. *Learning Theories for Teachers.* (3rd ed.) New York: Harper & Row, 1976.

Bischof, L. J. *Adult Psychology.* (2nd ed.) New York: Harper & Row, 1976.

Bock, L. K. "Participation." In A. B. Knox and Associates, *Developing, Administering, and Evaluating Adult Education.* San Francisco: Jossey-Bass, 1980.

Bohm, D. *Wholeness and the Implicate Order.* London: Routledge & Kegan Paul, 1980.

Boyd, R. D., Apps, J. W., and Associates. *Redefining the Discipline of Adult Education.* San Francisco: Jossey-Bass, 1980.

Boyer, E. "Higher Education Should Do More than Imitate Its Corporate Rivals." *Chronicle of Higher Education,* May 25, 1983, p. 32.

Brameld, T. *Education as Power.* New York: Holt, Rinehart and Winston, 1965.

Brauner, C., and Burns, H. *Problems in Education and Philosophy.* Englewood Cliffs, N.J.: Prentice-Hall, 1965.

Bridges, W. *Transitions.* Reading, Mass.: Addison-Wesley, 1980.

Brim, O. G., Jr. "Theories of the Male Mid-Life Crisis." *Counseling Psychologist,* 1976, *6*(1), 2-8.

Bromley, D. B. *The Psychology of Human Aging.* New York: Penguin Books, 1966.

Broudy, H. S. "How Philosophical Can Philosophy of Education Be?" *Journal of Philosophy,* 1955, *52,* 612-622.

Bruyn, S. T. *The Human Perspective in Sociology.* Englewood Cliffs, N.J.: Prentice-Hall, 1966.

Bryson, L. "Bridging the Gap." *Journal of Adult Education,* 1931, *3*(2), 161-164.

Buhler, C. "The Human Life Cycle as a Psychological Problem." In C. Buhler and F. Massarik (eds.), *The Course of Human Life.* New York: Springer, 1968. (Originally published 1933.)

Capra, F. *The Tao of Physics.* New York: Bantam Books, 1975.

Capra, F. *The Turning Point.* New York: Bantam Books, 1983.

Carlson, R. "Adult Education and Learning Theory: A Philosophical Concern." *Adult Leadership,* March 1972, p. 320.

Carstensen, V. "The Emergence of the Wisconsin Idea." In *The Wisconsin Idea: A Tribute to Carlisle P. Runge.* Madison: University of Wisconsin Extension, 1981.

Cattell, R. B. "Theory of Fluid and Crystallized Intelligence: A Critical Experiment." *Journal of Educational Psychology,* 1963, *54,* 1-22.

Cavalieri, L. F. *The Double-Edged Helix.* New York: Columbia University Press, 1981.

Collins, M. "A Critical Analysis of Competency-Based Systems in Adult Education." *Adult Education,* 1983, *33*(3), 174-183.

Cooperative Extension Service. *Extension in the '80s.* A Report of the Joint U.S. Department of Agriculture–NASULGC Committee on the Future of Cooperative Extension. Madison: Program Development and Evaluation of the Cooperative Extension Service, University of Wisconsin, May 1983.

Cotton, W. E. *On Behalf of Adult Education: A Historical Examination of the Supporting Literature.* Brookline, Mass.: Center for the Study of Liberal Education for Adults, 1968.

Cousins, N. "The End of Allusion." *Saturday Review,* May-June 1983, p. 4.

Creese, J. *The Extension of University Teaching.* New York: American Association for Adult Education, 1941.

Cross, K. P. *Adults as Learners: Increasing Participation and Facilitating Learning.* San Francisco: Jossey-Bass, 1981.

Daloz, L. "Returning to the Ways of the 1950's Isn't How to Prepare for the 1990's." *Chronicle of Higher Education,* September 14, 1983, p. 34.

Deardon, R. F. "Needs in Education." In M. Levit (ed.), *Curriculum: Readings in Philosophy of Education.* Urbana: University of Illinois Press, 1971.

Dennehy, R. "Education, Vocationalism and Democracy." *Thought,* 1982, *57*(225), 182-195.

Dewey, J. *How We Think.* Chicago: Henry Regnery, 1933.

Dewey, J. "Philosophy, Education, and Reflective Thinking." In T. O. Buford, *Toward a Philosophy of Education.* New York: Holt, Rinehart and Winston, 1969. (Originally published 1934.)

Edelman, M. *Political Language: Words That Succeed and Policies That Fail.* New York: Academic Press, 1977.

Elias, J. L., and Merriam, S. *Philosophical Foundations of Adult Education.* Huntington, N.Y.: Krieger, 1980.

Erikson, E. H. *Childhood and Society.* (2nd ed.) New York: Norton, 1963.

Farlow, H. *Publicizing and Promoting Programs.* New York: McGraw-Hill, 1979.

Fearnside, W. *About Thinking.* Englewood Cliffs, N.J.: Prentice-Hall, 1980.

Ferguson, M. *The Aquarian Conspiracy.* Los Angeles: Tarcher, 1980.

Fisher, D. C. *Why Stop Learning?* New York: Harcourt Brace Jovanovich, 1927.

Frandson, P. E. "The Politics of Continuing Education." *Continuum Quarterly,* 1979, *43*(4), 12-14.

Frankl, V. *Man's Search for Meaning.* New York: Beacon Press, 1963.

Freire, P. *Pedagogy of the Oppressed.* New York: Herder and Herder, 1970.

Freire, P. *Education for Critical Consciousness.* New York: Seabury Press, 1973.

Freud, S. *On Creativity and the Unconscious.* New York: Harper & Row, 1958. (Originally published 1925.)

Freud, S. *Civilization and Its Discontents.* New York: Norton, 1961. (Originally published 1930.)

Fromm, E. *The Revolution of Hope.* New York: Harper & Row, 1968.

Gagné, R. M. *The Conditions of Learning.* (3rd ed.) New York: Holt, Rinehart and Winston, 1977.

Geertz, C. *Local Knowledge.* New York: Basic Books, 1983.

Gilbert, J. G. "Thirty-five-Year Follow-Up Study of Intellectual Functioning." *Journal of Gerontology,* 1973, *28*(1), 68-72.

Goldberg, P. *The Intuitive Edge.* Los Angeles: Tarcher, 1983.

Gould, R. *Transformations.* New York: Simon & Schuster, 1978.

Grabowski, S. M. "Approaching Needs Assessments." In C. Klevins (ed.), *Materials and Methods in Adult and Continuing Education.* Los Angeles: Klevins, 1982.

Grattan, C. H. *In Quest of Knowledge: A Historical Perspective in Adult Education.* New York: Association Press, 1955.

Greene, M. *Teacher as Stranger.* Belmont, Calif.: Wadsworth, 1973.

Gueulette, D. (ed.). *Microcomputers for Adult Learning.* Chicago: Follett, 1982.

Habermas, J. *Knowledge and Human Interests.* Boston: Beacon Press, 1972.

Hall, J. C. "Staffing." In A. B. Knox and Associates, *Developing, Administering, and Evaluating Adult Education.* San Francisco: Jossey-Bass, 1980.

Harris, C. (ed.). *Encyclopedia of Educational Research.* (3rd ed.) New York: Macmillan, 1960.

Havighurst, R. J. "Changing Status and Roles During the Adult Life Cycle: Significance for Adult Education." In H. Burns (ed.), *Sociological Backgrounds of Adult Education.* Chicago: Center for the Study of Liberal Education of Adults, 1963.

Havighurst, R. J. *Developmental Tasks and Education.* (3rd ed.) New York: McKay, 1972.

Hostler, J. *The Aims of Adult Education.* Manchester, England: University of Manchester, 1981.

Houle, C. O. *The Design of Education.* San Francisco: Jossey-Bass, 1972.

Houle, C. O. *Continuing Learning in the Professions.* San Francisco: Jossey-Bass, 1980.

Hudson, J. W. *The History of Adult Education.* New York: Augustus M. Kelly, 1969. (Originally published 1851.)

Huebner, D. "Curricular Language and Classroom Meanings." In J. MacDonald and R. R. Leeper (eds.), *Language and Meaning.* Washington, D.C.: Association for Supervision and Curriculum Development, 1966.

Illich, I. *Deschooling Society.* New York: Harper & Row, 1971.

Illich, I. "Silence in a Commons." *CoEvolution Quarterly,* Winter 1983, pp. 5-9.

Jantsch, E. *Design for Evolution.* New York: Braziller, 1975.

Jensen, G., Liveright, A., and Hallenbeck, W. (eds.). *Adult Education: Outlines of an Emerging Field of University Study.* Washington, D.C.: Adult Education Association of the U.S.A., 1964.

Johnstone, J. W., and Rivera, R. J. *Volunteers for Learning.* Chicago: Aldine, 1965.

Kasworm, C. E., and Anderson, C. A. "Perceptions of Decision Makers." In D. G. Gueulette, *Microcomputers for Adult Learning.* Chicago: Follett, 1982.

Keddie, N. "Adult Education: An Ideology of Individualism." In J. Thompson, *Adult Education for a Change.* London: Hutchinson, 1980.

Kliebard, H. M. "Bureaucracy and Curriculum Theory." In V. Haubich (ed.), *Freedom, Bureaucracy, and Schooling.* Washington, D.C.: Association for Supervision and Curriculum Development, 1971.

Kliebard, H. M. "Reappraisal: The Tyler Rationale." In W. Pinar (ed.), *Curriculum Theorizing: The Reconceptualists.* Berkeley, Calif.: McCutchan, 1975.

Knowles, M. *Self-Directed Learning.* New York: Cambridge University Press, 1975.

Knowles, M. *The Modern Practice of Adult Education.* Chicago: Follett, 1980.

Knox, A. B. *Adult Development and Learning: A Handbook on*

Individual Growth and Competence in the Adult Years. San Francisco: Jossey-Bass, 1977.

Kotler, P. *Marketing For Non Profit Organizations.* Englewood Cliffs, N.J.: Prentice-Hall, 1975.

Krishnamurti, J. *Education and the Significance of Life.* New York: Harper & Row, 1953.

Krishnamurti, J. *Krishnamurti on Education.* New York: Harper & Row, 1974.

Kuhn, T. *The Structure of Scientific Revolutions.* (2nd ed.) Chicago: University of Chicago Press, 1970.

Langer, S. K. "Philosophy and Education." *Harvard Educational Review,* 1956, *26,* 139-141.

Levinson, D. J. *The Seasons of a Man's Life.* New York: Knopf, 1978.

Lindeman, E. C. *The Meaning of Adult Education.* Montreal: Harvest House, 1961. (Originally published 1926.)

Lloyd, A. S. "Critical Consciousness and Adult Education: An Exploratory Study of Freire's Concept of Conscientization." Unpublished master's thesis, University of Wisconsin-Madison, 1974.

Lyons, W. "You Asked About Philosophy." *Teaching Philosophy,* 1982, *5*(3), 227-233.

McCall, R. *Basic Logic.* (2nd ed.) New York: Barnes & Noble, 1952.

Machan, T. *Introduction to Philosophical Inquiries.* Boston: Allyn & Bacon, 1977.

McKenzie, L. *Adult Education and the Burden of the Future.* Washington, D.C.: University Press of America, 1978.

McPeck, J. "Critical Thinking Without Logic: Restoring Dignity to Information." *Philosophy of Education, 1981 Proceedings of the Philosophy of Education Society,* April 26-29, 1981, pp. 219-227.

Mager, R. F. *Preparing Instructional Objectives.* Belmont, Calif.: Pitman Learning, 1962.

Marris, P. *Loss and Change.* London: Routledge & Kegan Paul, 1974.

Martin, E. D. "Wanted: Enlightenment!" *Journal of Adult Education,* 1932, *4*(3), 291-294.

Maslow, A. H. *Toward a Psychology of Being.* New York: Van Nostrand Reinhold, 1968.

Maslow, A. H. *Motivation and Personality.* (2nd ed.) New York: Harper & Row, 1970.

Matson, F. *The Idea of Man.* New York: Dell, 1976.

Merriam, S. "Middle Age: A Review of the Research." In A. B. Knox (ed.), *Programming for Adults Facing Mid-Life Change.* New Directions for Continuing Education, no. 2. San Francisco: Jossey-Bass, 1979.

Meyers, J. G. "Grieving and Small Group Phase Development." Unpublished manuscript, University of Wisconsin–Madison, 1984.

Mezirow, J. "A Critical Theory of Adult Learning and Education." *Adult Education,* 1981, *32*(1), 3–24.

Moenster, P. A. "Learning and Memory in Relation to Age." *Journal of Gerontology,* 1972, *27,* 361–363.

Monette, M. "The Concept of Educational Need: An Analysis of Selected Literature." *Adult Education,* 1977, *28*(2), 116–127.

Monette, M. "Need Assessment: A Critique of Philosophical Assumptions." *Adult Education,* 1979, *29*(2), 83–95.

Moore, B. *Philosophy Applied to Controversial Issues in a Democratic Society.* Washington, D.C.: University Press of America, 1979.

Morrison, J. "Continuing Education and the Making of Public Policy." *Continuum Quarterly,* 1979, *43*(4), 5–6.

Murchland, B. "Technology, Liberal Learning, and Civic Purpose." *Liberal Education,* Winter 1982, pp. 297–309.

Naisbitt, J. *Megatrends.* New York: Warner Books, 1982.

National Commission on Excellence in Education. *A Nation at Risk: The Imperative for Educational Reform.* Washington, D.C.: National Commission on Excellence in Education, 1983.

Neugarten, B. L. "Personality and Aging." In J. E. Birren and K. W. Schaie (eds.), *Handbook of the Psychology of Aging.* New York: Van Nostrand Reinhold, 1977.

Nisbet, R. *Social Change and History.* London: Oxford University Press, 1969.

Nowlen, P. M. "Program Origins." In A. B. Knox and Associates, *Developing, Administering, and Evaluating Adult Education.* San Francisco: Jossey-Bass, 1980.

Ohliger, J. "Is Lifelong Adult Education a Guarantee of Permanent Inadequacy?" *Convergence,* 1974, 7(2), 52.

Ohliger, J. "Prospects for a Learning Society." *Adult Leadership,* September 1975, pp. 37-39.

Ommen, J., Brainard, W., and Canfield, A. "Learning Preferences of Young and Older Students." *Community College Frontiers,* 1979, 7(3), 29-33.

Ornstein, R. *The Mind Field.* New York: Pocket Books, 1976.

Ortega y Gasset, J. *What Is Philosophy?* New York: Norton, 1960.

Packard, V. *The Hidden Persuaders.* New York: McKay, 1957.

Papert, S. A. "Computers and Learning." In M. Dertouszos and J. Moses (eds.), *The Computer Age: A Twenty-Year View.* Cambridge: MIT Press, 1980.

Paterson, R. W. K. *Values, Education and the Adult.* London: Routledge & Kegan Paul, 1979.

Pennington, F., and Green, J. "Comparative Analysis of Program Development Processes in Six Professions." *Adult Education,* 1976, 27(1), 13-23.

Peters, T. J., and Waterman, R. H., Jr. *In Search of Excellence.* New York: Harper & Row, 1982.

Reid, A. "Philosophy and the Theory and Practice of Education." In R. D. Archambault (ed.), *Philosophical Analysis and Education.* New York: Humanities Press, 1972.

Richer, S. "Toward a Radical Pedagogy." *Interchange,* 1981-82, 12(4), 46-63.

Robinson, R. *An Introduction to Helping Adults Learn and Change.* Milwaukee, Wisc.: Omnibook, 1979.

Rogers, C. *On Becoming a Person.* Boston: Houghton Mifflin, 1961.

Rogers, C. *Freedom to Learn.* Columbus, Ohio: Merrill, 1969.

Roth, E. "APL: A Ferment in Education." *American Education,* 1976, 12(4), 6-10.

Savićević, D. M. *The Man and Life-Long Education.* Titograd: Republicki zavod za Unapredivanje Skolstva, 1983.

Schaie, K. W., and Geiwitz, J. *Adult Development and Aging.* Boston: Little, Brown, 1982.

Schaie, K. W., and Parr, J. "Intelligence." In A. W. Chickering and Associates, *The Modern American College: Responding to the New Realities of Diverse Students and a Changing Society.* San Francisco: Jossey-Bass, 1981.

Scheffler, I. *The Language of Education.* Springfield, Ill.: Thomas, 1960.

Shannon, T. J., and Schoenfeld, C. A. *University Extension.* New York: Center for Applied Research in Education, 1965.

Sheehy, G. *Passages.* New York: Dutton, 1976.

Simon, H. A. *The Sciences of the Artificial.* Cambridge: MIT Press, 1969.

Simpson, E. L. "Program Development: A Model." In C. Klevins (ed.), *Materials and Methods in Adult and Continuing Education.* Los Angeles: Klevins, 1982.

Singarella, T., and Sork, T. "Questions of Values and Conduct: Ethical Issues for Adult Education." *Adult Education Quarterly,* 1983, *33*(4), 244–251.

Skinner, B. F. *Science and Human Behavior.* New York: Macmillan, 1953.

Smith, R. (ed.). *Thinking, Knowing, Living: An Introduction.* Washington, D.C.: University Press of America, 1978.

Smith, R. *Learning How to Learn.* Chicago: Follett, 1982.

Snow, C. P. *The Two Cultures and the Scientific Revolution.* London: Cambridge University Press, 1959.

Spiegelberg, H. *Doing Phenomenology.* The Hague: Martinus Nijhoff, 1975.

Sullivan, H. S. *Clinical Studies in Psychiatry.* New York: Norton, 1956.

Thorndike, E. L. *The Fundamentals of Learning.* New York: Teachers College, Columbia University, 1932.

Toffler, A. *The Third Wave.* New York: William Morrow, 1980.

Tough, A. *The Adult's Learning Projects.* Toronto: Ontario Institute for Studies in Education, 1971.

Tuan, Y.-F. *Segmented Worlds and Self.* Minneapolis: University of Minnesota Press, 1982.

Tyler, R. *Basic Principles of Curriculum and Instruction.* Chicago: University of Chicago Press, 1950.

von Oech, R. *A Whack on the Side of the Head.* New York: Warner, 1983.

Wallas, G. *The Art of Thought.* New York: Harcourt Brace Jovanovich, 1926.

Wear, R. "Beware the New Carthaginians." *Chronicle of Higher Education,* September 12, 1977, p. 32.

Wechsler, D. *The Measurement and Appraisal of Adult Intelligence.* (3rd ed.) Baltimore, Md.: Williams & Wilkins, 1972.

Wedemeyer, C. *Learning at the Back Door.* Madison: University of Wisconsin Press, 1981.

Weizenbaum, J. "Once More: The Computer Revolution." In M. Dertouszos and J. Moses (eds.), *The Computer Age: A Twenty-Year View.* Cambridge: MIT Press, 1980.

Weston, A. "A Pattern for Argument Analysis in Informal Logic." *Teaching Philosophy,* 1982, *5*(2), 135-139.

Wicklein, J. *Electronic Nightmare.* New York: Viking Press, 1979.

Wilbur, K. (ed.). *The Holographic Paradigm and Other Paradoxes.* Boulder, Colo.: Shambhala, 1982.

Wolcott, H. F. "The Anthropology of Learning." *Anthropology and Education Quarterly,* 1982, *13*(2), 83-108.

Yeaxlee, B. *An Educated Nation.* New York: Oxford University Press, 1921.

Zukav, G. *The Dancing Wu Li Masters.* New York: William Morrow, 1979.

Zwerling, L. S. "Adult Education: Breeder of Inequality?" *New York Times,* August 22, 1982, Education Section, p. 49.

Index

221

IMPROVING PRACTICE IN CONTINUING EDUCATION

Many continuing education practitioners are asking fundamental questions today about what they are doing and why. They recognize that current practices must be examined, evaluated, and, in some cases, challenged. In his new book, Jerold Apps provides a systematic and comprehensive approach for understanding the field, improving programs and practices, and making future decisions.

He explains how to conduct evaluations in each of five areas: adult learning needs, goals for continuing education programs, teaching and learning techniques, program content and development, and policy making. And he specifies how to use a variety of methods of analysis to evaluate all aspects of continuing education programs, from general educational direction and aims to budget and staffing decisions.

With the concrete program evaluation procedures offered in the book, practitioners can examine program development strategies critically and broaden the program approaches they use. Apps details how to identify, analyze, and assess the assumptions, definitions, and aims of continuing education in general and of specific programs. And he examines how to evaluate the needs of today's adult learners and